WHY
EVERYTHING
THAT DOESN'T
MATTER,
MATTERS
SO MUCH

WHY EVERYTHING THAT DOESN'T MATTER, MATTERS SO MUCH

the WAY of LOVE in a WORLD of HURT

CHARLIE PEACOCK and ANDI ASHWORTH

W PUBLISHING GROUP

AN IMPRINT OF THOMAS NELSON

Published in Nashville, Tennessee, by W Publishing, an imprint of Thomas Nelson.

Published in association with Don Pape of Pape Commons.

Thomas Nelson titles may be purchased in bulk for educational, business, fundraising, or sales promotional use. For information, please email SpecialMarkets@ThomasNelson.com.

Unless otherwise noted, Scripture quotations are taken from The Holy Bible, New International Version®, NIV®. Copyright © 1973, 1978, 1984, 2011 by Biblica, Inc.® Used by permission of Zondervan. All rights reserved worldwide. www.Zondervan.com. The "NIV" and "New International Version" are trademarks registered in the United States Patent and Trademark Office by Biblica, Inc.®

Scripture quotations marked MSG are taken from THE MESSAGE. Copyright © 1993, 2002, 2018 by Eugene H. Peterson. Used by permission of NavPress. All rights reserved. Represented by Tyndale House Publishers, Inc.

Any internet addresses, phone numbers, or company or product information printed in this book are offered as a resource and are not intended in any way to be or to imply an endorsement by Thomas Nelson, nor does Thomas Nelson vouch for the existence, content, or services of these sites, phone numbers, companies, or products beyond the life of this book.

ISBN 978-1-4003-3773-6 (audiobook)
ISBN 978-1-4003-3772-9 (ePub)
ISBN 978-1-4003-3764-4 (TP)

Library of Congress Control Number: 2023941157

Printed in the United States of America

23 24 25 26 27 LBC 5 4 3 2 1

*We dedicate this book to each other and
to our family: Molly, Mark, Robert, Sam,
Ruby, Brinsley, Alfie, and Bridget.*

Images of tiny things, babies, yeast and mustard seeds can guide us; things that grow are what change everything. Moments of compassion, giving, grief, and wonder shift our behavior, get inside us, and change realms we might not have agreed to have changed. Each field is weeds and wheat, but mix the wheat with yeast, the most ordinary of elements, and it starts changing the flour. It becomes bread and so do we, bread to eat and to offer. The world keeps going on. You can have yet another cup of coffee and keep working on your plans. Or you can take the risk to be changed, surrounded, and indwelled by this strange yeasty mash called mercy, there for the asking at the frog pond, the River Jordan, the channel that flows between the lagoon and the sea.[1]

—Anne Lamott

CONTENTS

CONTENTS

one

ON THE LOOKOUT
FOR REDEMPTION

To You, Dear Reader

from Andi & Charlie

Several years ago, a former high school classmate of ours was in Istanbul, Turkey, on vacation. She was sitting in her hotel room watching the international news when a segment on the Brazilian collector of vinyl records, Zero Freitas from São Paulo, came on. He's not just any collector. He's the biggest in the world. Zero has over two million albums in his collection, with nearly two hundred thousand of them digitized and fully cataloged in a massive São Paulo warehouse. At the close of the piece, the reporter pulled out one from the thousands of albums. And as our friend later shared in her Facebook post: "That album was none other than our own Charlie Peacock!"

São Paulo, or Saint Paul, was born in the Roman city of Tarsus on the Mediterranean coast of what is now Turkey. Paul, originally called Saul, was a chronic persecutor of Christians and was struck blind on the road to Damascus in Syria. After three days, a follower of Jesus named Ananias restored Paul's sight. Paul spent the remainder of his life on the road or in prison, spreading the teachings of Jesus in person and through letters.

We shared the Brazilian record collector story with our then nine-year-old grandson Alfie. He picked up on the word *Brazil*, saying: "I want to go to Brazil."

"Why?" we asked. "That's where the statue is," said Alfie. Ah yes, Christ the Redeemer.

We want to be where Christ the Redeemer is—we need that proximity, always. For us, it might be said that the whole of this life is either moving in the direction of Jesus and the redemption on offer, or away from it. There is no standing still.

Though our lives have seen both directions, we've overwhelmingly experienced the *toward* more than the *away*, always closer, if never fully arriving. Our lives brim with grace.

When we were young and the whole world lay before us, we could not have predicted the story our life would become. Yes, there were prescient signs when we were teenagers. We met as freshmen in high school and by the summer we'd become an inseparable couple. We were a tangle of teenage love, self-reliance, trauma bond, hyper-vigilance, and dreams—lots of dreams.

We saw ourselves married, as parents, one a nurse, the other a poet. We shared the language of music, from Joni Mitchell to Miles Davis. Creative writing and journaling were our norm. Books were Ebenezer stones—serial helpers infusing our imaginations and changing the way we viewed the world.

During our sophomore year of high school, we entertained a mostly unreliable version of Christianity. This included spotty church attendance on our part and, for one of us, a brief interest in attending Bible college. Once or twice we might have prayed together. Then the interest waned and withered. Though we believed there was, in some inscrutable way, a creator God, the true nature of Jesus and his mission had escaped us. Or not been on offer at all.

Ten more years would pass before essential, trustworthy information about Jesus arrived at our doorstep. This was good news, just as the Bible claims it to be. Our need of grace, reconciliation, and forgiveness had become acute. Jesus was the lifesaving help we needed.

One among many songwriters we would host in our home in the coming years was David Wilcox. His song "Show the Way" asks the question: "If someone wrote a play / just to glorify what's stronger than hate / would they not arrange the stage / to look as if the hero came too late?"[1]

For us, it certainly looked that way. In reality, Jesus, the loving, empathetic hero, was always willing and waiting to do for us what we could not do for ourselves. As David sings, to "show the way."

From that time on, the Jesus way began its work in us. Call it the greatest life hack ever. Jesus rewrote our code. Over years, desiring what Martin Luther King Jr. called the beloved community, we incrementally discovered, understood, and became equipped to embody a new way to be human. Though we lived in it imperfectly, this pattern of community—also described by Wendell Berry as "common experience and common effort on a common ground to which one willingly belongs"[2]—continues to inspire and shape us.

As young people, like horse and rider, we rode the surface of our dreams and beliefs about what was real, just, and faithful. It was the best we could do at the time. As older adults, in the back third of life, dreams resist the superficial. As do most of our convictions and commitments. Intentionally and tacitly, we share the practice of the examined life. Maturity calls us to the deep end, not the shallow. Though history paints this as Socratic, it's also the way of Jesus—with one essential cosmic tweak.

For the follower of Jesus, the examined life is founded in the practice of carefully examining the life of Jesus. This is not a one-and-done effort. Instead, this is a lifelong work of study, application, and embodiment (otherwise known as discipleship). With Jesus in view, we are able to see ourselves and our world in the light of God's love and grace.

To the degree that we locate our identity and mission in these twin gifts of unconditional love and irreversible grace, to that degree we are free and at peace, able to do good work and to examine our lives with "sober judgment, in accordance with the faith God has distributed to each" of us (Romans 12:3).

The poet Mary Oliver's simple and profound "instructions for living" fit well here: "Pay attention. Be astonished. Tell about it."[3] This is the vocation we embrace.

The examined life means certain things for each of us: a psalm in the morning, an open journal once a week, a Bible marked from beginning to end with dates of passage, prayers throughout the day and night. We seek understanding by reading books and articles, listening to podcast interviews, staying alert to what's going on around us, and taking the testimony of the abused and oppressed seriously. Knowing others and being known by them is crucial. We place a high value on having honest conversations with friends, getting help from therapists, and working at our marriage all along the way. Vulnerability is key.

At times, we've longed for someone wise to come alongside and offer practical guidance. Maybe a person or a couple with the authority of age, who could understand all the pieces we were holding and speak into our reality. But instead of a few mentors, we've had so many that our hearts are full remembering them all.

We read their books, met them at retreats, and talked over bowls of homemade granola in our kitchen. No one had the same story we did. They didn't need to. We gathered up their words like nuggets of gold and carried them with us through our own unique experiences.

In our late twenties, along with our new belief in Jesus, we unknowingly entered the '80s evangelical subculture. For all that was redemptive, there was an equal measure of extraneous belief and behavior to sift through, question, and ultimately reject. We learned difficult (and often embarrassing) lessons. Without wisdom and discernment, we could too easily find ourselves associating with a form of Christianity bearing little resemblance to the way of Jesus. Staying watchful and informed became an essential safeguard.

For example, early on we picked up a way of thinking common to our Christian community: *We're heading toward eternity. This earth, this life, and what we do in it are secondary in importance.* We're just passing through. With this mindset, one of us quit taking college classes, while the other almost set aside music to explore Bible college. Thankfully, corrective help was on the way.

It began with Edith Schaeffer books discovered in a church library. Her stories of L'Abri in Switzerland and *Art and the Bible*, a small booklet written by her husband, Francis, corrected our course. Our minds and hearts expanded as we embraced the mantra that *all of life matters to God*. The Schaeffers and those who came after them inspired us to care, to learn about the world with the same enthusiasm we had to learn from the Bible. The goal? To cultivate a life of the mind while being firmly planted in our flesh-and-bone, earthly existence.

We experienced the good of asking honest questions, talking about everything over meals and in our living room. Francis Schaeffer's phrase "there are no little people and no little places" and Mother Teresa's "small things with great love" are always in the back of our minds. They taught us that valuing the individual is the Jesus way. Every person is made in the image of God and has infinite worth. Our friends Denis and Margie Haack (writers with a long vocation in hospitality and teaching) emphasized faithfulness in the ordinary, "even though your ordinary may be far different from mine."[4]

As our own lives unfolded, we were able to get in the flow, in part because of those who had come before us, and those we'd meet along the way. We wanted to care, to contribute, to help people create on the world's stages and in the details of ordinary life. Making homes, making music, making memories—everything is shot through with meaning. Beauty matters! So does governing, science, medicine, farming, and waiting tables! This is our Creator's world. It is joyful and serious business to live in it.

When Os Guinness's book *The Call* arrived on the scene in 1998, we devoured it. We took his words into our lives and made them our own: "God calls us to himself so decisively that everything we are, everything we do, and everything we have is invested with a special devotion and dynamism lived out of a response to his summons and service."[5] As with so many of our influences, Os's summary words gave us the encouragement to live for God and people, everywhere (place), and in everything (vocation).

As we've followed the trail of our given lives, with all this mattering and meaning, we've learned the need to focus, to think together about desires, limitations, and our small and large imaginings for what is yet to be. We think about what it means to gift others with what we have received and with all we continue to hope for.

Study the methods and habits of writers and you quickly learn that the spectrum of why and how people write is quite broad. Granted, most writing exists to tell a story, inform, describe, or convince. But there's a fraction that exists for all of these and another, lesser-known motivation: writing as a way of knowing. Both of us fit into this writing-as-epistemology model. We write to know what we know.

It's through writing about a subject that we come to understand something or someone more clearly. We read and study, listen and converse, and, as a result, learn. But nothing helps us sort out self, neighbor, and the world more than writing. The act of writing is story and assessment, a way of bearing witness, a means of organizing convictions and commitments, and a documentation of all that love values—as we incrementally come to understand this more clearly, year after year.

We started the practice of writing family letters when our children were young. Once a year for Valentine's Day, each of us wrote a love letter to the other three and read them aloud after dinner. We continued the tradition for special occasions: Sam's graduation from high school, Molly's graduation from college, both kids' fortieth birthdays. Now we write a letter to our grandchildren when they turn thirteen. Three have received their letters. There's one more to go. We want them to know: These are the gifts and abilities we've seen growing in you. We delight in who you are. We see the ways you love. We're cheering you on!

To one grandchild, we wrote about his grand imagination, his loving-kindness and affectionate ways, his gifts of art, design, and writing. "You pay attention to who people are and what they love, caring about them through what you make." To another, we noted her beautiful, strong singing voice, love for books, her abilities in the visual arts, and her joy and skill with baking. To the third child, we talked about his brave, adventuresome spirit, his athletic gifts (which include climbing to the top of tall trees and doing backflips in the yard!), and his knowledge of how things work. At thirteen he was already a genius at taking people's discarded junk and electronics and creating amazing new inventions. And though our fourth grandchild is only twelve, if we were writing her letter right now, we'd tell her how sharp, observant, and witty she is. She creates artful jewelry, is a thoughtful gift maker, and is her grandmother's trusted sous chef. We'd say, "Your original songs have the power of good pop music. Keep writing and performing!"

All of this naming is only the beginning, but we want to affirm the beautiful things we've seen already. As our grandchildren grow into the years, their personalities, gifts, interests, families, circumstances, and sufferings will shape who they are and how they care. The sum of how they care will become their unique contribution to people and place.

So now we carry on writing about our life together, offering these letters to you, dear reader, hoping it will be clear what we mean when we profess to be students and followers of Jesus. Though this claim has become nearly meaningless in this day of competing Christian narratives, we still claim it as our act of faith, of moving our imperfect selves toward the redemption he extends to all. No Christian should want anything less than the gospel framed, lived, and modeled by Jesus.

Though far from exhaustive or perfect, we hope these letters reveal something of how we view our individual vocations, the general vocation of humanity at work and play in the world, and specifically what we believe to be the mission of every person who professes to follow Jesus. We know the good fruit of having trustworthy guides help us navigate life and hope that our collected writings will have like effect. In these letters, we are simply passing on what others passed to us. That is, sharing our story and how our understanding of a Jesus-centric life has shaped us and continues to fuel our vision for life and love.

In these letters you'll read about gardening, citizenship, writing and reading, cooking, suffering, serving, education, and music-making—and the creation of family life. We share our practices of journaling, praying, and calling upon love and the good imagination to energize our creativity. This mix of topics (and much more) bears witness to our conviction that everything matters to God. We know the voices that whisper and shout, telling us this or that doesn't really matter much—*it's a small thing of little importance.* Don't believe it. After a long life of wildly diverse experiences, inhabiting a huge, Creator-centric story, we know it's often the smallest things that matter most. Neutrality of word and deed is a myth. A former classmate watching a television show in Istanbul, Turkey, about a Brazilian record collector can seamlessly lead to a conversation with a grandchild about a statue named Christ the Redeemer, in a city named after Saint Paul, a man born in Turkey. Stranger things have happened.

In many ways, the content of the letters and our daily practices matured and bore fruit in the context of a nonprofit we founded in Nashville called the Art House, now with branches in Saint Paul and Dallas. Over the years, one of the Art House phrases that's stuck with us is "the artful, faithful life." We dig into the details of how we define this pursuit and how we've tried to embody it in daily life and within the communities we've served and have membership in.

To you, beloved reader, we say, be on the lookout for redemption. It comes in waves. God moves in love. As Switchfoot sang, "Love is the movement." A movement we promote. Not as a means of reducing the complexities of our world to sloganeering. But rather, reminding ourselves and listening communities that love is the highest way of knowing and the trustworthy basis of imaginative and creative good. Love is not abstract. To us, life is defined as *the way of love*. How we define and embody love is evidence of what we value, what we treasure. It says something concrete about how we view humanity, the earth, and our part in the unfolding story. And the way of love is the only trustworthy antidote for the world of hurt inside us, and outside our doorsteps.

Our conviction is that the Creator of the universe has entrusted Jesus with everyone and everything that must be kept safe in his wide-open arms. And all that must be kept safe is simply all that love values. As the hymn sings: "O love that will not let me go / I rest my weary soul in thee. / I give thee back the life I owe, / that in thine ocean depths its flow, / may richer, fuller be."[6] All that love values is a mirror of all that Jesus will not let go. From São Paulo to Nashville.

two

WHY BOTHER LEARNING TO COOK

To Those Who Hunger and Thirst for Something More

from Andi

I remember all the days when cooking was about more than food. I can almost taste them still. And I found words that named something important on the day when Bridget (my then twelve-year-old granddaughter) was dropped off early to help me cook for a family dinner. Her first job was to make buttercream frosting and decorate the birthday cakes—one for her little sister, Brinsley, and one for her cousin Robert. With bowls of colored frosting and piping bags for the detail work, Bridget was deep in concentration.

When she finished, we prepped for dinner—chopping, dicing, and sautéing, the scent of minced garlic and fresh basil filling the room. Standing at the cutting board, she quietly murmured, "The sounds of the kitchen are so satisfying." It was an insightful thing for a child to say, and I wrote it in my journal to keep for her. It was clear even then that cooking and baking—among her many artistic gifts— are part of the puzzle of what matters to her.

For some of us, cooking is an essential part of our skill set and our creative work. It's part of our calling. Our imagination traffics in food. Like Bridget, we love the sounds of the kitchen. We like cookbooks, pots and pans, mixing bowls, and our favorite spatulas. With a little experience, we learn to dig deeper in our kitchens and use what's at hand. With some butter, sugar, flour, and eggs, we can make a dessert. Or turn a can of crushed tomatoes, some white beans, the last onion, a bit of broth, and a few vegetable remnants into a soup. Dust the finished bowls of soup with Parmesan. Voilà, you have a meal!

But even if cooking is not our thing, we still need to eat. Learning how to cook, whether just the basics or more elaborately, will take us all the way through a hungry life. With a little or a lot, we can feed ourselves and care for others, responding to the moment we're in. I haven't always known that.

On a recent visit with my friend Kate, as our conversation moved between books and family news, we talked of how one person's skill and memory can become someone else's skill and memory, sometimes unawares. My mind traveled to my grandmother's tiny kitchen table in the 1960s, curtains open, soft light filling the room. A grandmother and her grandchild doing the most ordinary, accessible thing—talking and making cookies, orange slice cookies, a classic in those days.

With a mixing bowl between us, my grandmother stood on one side of the table measuring ingredients: eggs, butter, white and brown sugar, vanilla, flour, baking powder and baking soda, coconut, and quick-cooking oats. Across from her, I dipped a dull paring knife in flour and cut orange slice candies into pieces, adding them to the mixture and stirring with a wooden spoon. This memory never leaves me. It's cemented in my brain. Of the many things I learned at that kitchen table, I experienced food and its creation as a kind of love that satisfied many kinds of hungers.

At the mention of my grandmother, Kate said she'd been thinking about food and memory just a few days before. "I was making the frittatas I learned from you in the Art House kitchen in 2007! You told me then, 'When you need to make breakfast for a crowd, frittatas are the way to go. Bacon and potato frittatas. Prosciutto, asparagus, and goat cheese frittatas. Or any combination of sautéed vegetables and cheese you like. Make them in a half sheet pan and cut in squares. Serve on a platter, warm or at room temperature.'"

You never know what someone is picking up when you're in the kitchen together. I got the frittata recipe from my friend Kathi, a chef who is generous with her knowledge. For years, I've called her for ideas and instructions. How do you cook a leg of lamb? What's the correct temperature for a roasted pork loin? What can I make to serve forty-five people for a large breakfast gathering? Frittatas.

Her basic recipe became essential in my cooking repertoire. I've cut it in half, and I've multiplied it times two, using forty eggs instead of the original twenty. I've made it for baby showers, family gatherings, and large Art House events. My daughter, Molly, uses it. Local friends have used it. This is the beauty of food knowledge, given freely and passed from person to person, generation to generation.

But how does one get from here to there—from having no cooking experience to caring for people in family life and hospitality, to cooking through challenging passages of our history? I will tell you my story.

(Note to the reader: I call my husband "Chuck" because that's what his family and friends called him when we met. The name "Charlie" came later, in our early twenties.)

The first meal Chuck and I made together after we married in May 1975 was a dinner of orange Jell-O and canned asparagus. We'd decided to be vegetarians but had no idea how to go about it in a healthy way. At the ages of eighteen and nineteen, we knew very little about good nutrition and even less about whole foods. As a result, on our first food-gathering trip to Albertsons, we simply left the meat out of the grocery cart and came home with foods that were familiar to us.

I left my mother's home knowing almost nothing about cooking, or why it would matter to learn. Other than making cookie dough or occasionally starting the meatloaf before she got home from work, I was largely ignorant of the culinary arts. It was a loss. I could have learned so much.

My mom was an excellent cook. She baked the best apple pies I've ever eaten, fried chicken to perfection, slow-cooked pans of succulent and saucy spareribs, and made mouth-watering penuche on Christmas Eve.

When her own mom died of a stroke after a long battle with heart disease, my eleven-year-old mother learned to cook for her father and little brother. She would call her mother's friend for instructions. Until two years later when my grandfather married the grandmother I knew and loved, Mom was given all responsibility for the household. It was a heavy load for a child to carry, especially in 1941 when housework was so labor-intensive. Schoolwork and grief weighed her down even more. Ever the hard worker, my mother was resourceful and did what she needed to do. She told me once, "We had lots of pork and beans and chocolate pudding because those were the two things I could make well. We didn't have much meat in those days, though—sometimes chicken, but always those canned pork and beans."

My mother married my father the minute she graduated from high school. Twelve years later she divorced him on the grounds of extreme cruelty. I was four and a half. I struggle to use those words because you never want to define someone at their worst, but they were in the newspaper, in the stories that came to me in bits and pieces over decades. They explain so much about how his life played out and the string of hurting family members left in the wake.

The complexity of Mom's pain caused more pain. Her second marriage produced an intensity of damaging consequences for my sister Paula and me. There was so much that was wrong. Even with years of therapy behind me, I am left with questions and no one to ask. For all that I cannot unravel or understand, mercy.

The blessing of the marriage was an older stepsister whom I loved and who loved me. She brought me leftover Shakey's pizza after her dates and lent me her Beatles records.

Though Mom loved her work and hung in for the long haul, eventually becoming executive secretary to the president of a contracting company, she was anxious and worried, constantly on the move to maintain order. When she arrived home each day, she was rushed as she moved straight into the second shift—dinner, dishes, bills. It was hard for her to sit still. She rarely smiled.

Later in life, when I wondered why I hadn't learned more from my mother while I had the chance, I realized I hadn't been invited in. Or had I missed the cue? She did her time-consuming cooking on the weekends, but after assigning us a light amount of housework on Saturdays, my sisters and I were set free. She said we'd have enough household responsibility when we were adults. She didn't want to burden us when we were young.

All of that changed when I announced at the age of nineteen that I was getting married. Suddenly it mattered that I could feed myself when I left home. In the months leading up to my wedding, Mom ordered the Betty Crocker Recipe Card Library, which arrived by mail in monthly installments. I loved receiving those packages and would sit on the couch looking intently through each set of recipes, the categories ranging from Budget Casseroles to Fondues to Family Breakfast Brighteners. Then I tucked them away in the green plastic box provided for their storage and there they stayed, with the exception of the recipe for crème wafers—delicate, frosted sandwich cookies that I made and gave to Chuck for Valentine's Day. I was intrigued by the possibilities for cooking, but as a budding young feminist, I was more taken with discussions about equitable distributions of kitchen labor than I was with casseroles.

It never occurred to me to think of cooking as an important skill to possess, or how it could figure into the flourishing of human life and be used in the service of others.

Thankfully, for our nutritional well-being, the first house Chuck and I rented in Marysville, California, was only a few blocks away from the original site of Sunflower Natural Foods, a wonderful grocery store and lunch counter. There, we had our first taste of natural food classics—mushroom burgers and sandwiches made with whole grain bread, jack cheese, fresh tomatoes, avocados, and sprouts. As we roamed the aisles and became acquainted with new foods, we were captured by the unending possibilities for creating good meals.

While browsing the store on one of our first visits, we picked up two small paperbacks: *Diet for a Small Planet* and *Recipes for a Small Planet*. We began learning to combine grains, legumes, seeds, and dairy products to produce complete proteins and a healthier vegetarian diet. We also started cooking from the recipes. We still have the books. Our favorites from those days are dog-eared and splashed with forty-eight-year-old food stains. We loved egg and soy grit tacos, vegetarian enchiladas, and chocolate chip cookies made with whole wheat flour, peanuts, and sunflower seeds.

One night we invited my sister and brother-in-law for dinner and cooked them one of our best dishes, mushrooms supreme. Resembling a heavy soufflé, it's made with mushrooms, onions, whole wheat flour, milk, and eggs. There was nothing too esoteric about the recipe, but it was not what our family was used to. We still tease our brother-in-law—meat lover that he was and is—for leaving our house and heading straight to the nearest hamburger joint!

––––––

Learning about food was part of my becoming interested in the wider world and beginning a more concentrated search for meaning. Inside the yellow walls of our first home, we set apart one portion of our bedroom to practice meditation and furnished it with a throw rug, two large pillows, a Buddha incense holder, and an orange crate to use as a bookshelf. Our tiny library of books and magazines reflected the times as well as our growing interests. There were stacks of *Ms.* magazines, poetry by Gary Snyder, Jack Kerouac's *On the Road*, the *Whole Earth Catalog*, *Tao Te Ching*, and Kate Millett's *Sexual Politics*. We sat cross-legged on the pillows, discussing ideas and eating sautéed vegetables over brown rice, feeling the camaraderie of being together in the world with our whole lives in front of us.

As we explored the ideas and art of our culture, we went to concerts, films, poetry readings, and lectures sponsored by the National Organization for Women.

We drove to San Francisco to hear the best jazz artists play at the Great American Music Hall. And we continued to experiment with food. But we were also experimenting with other things that would turn the next years increasingly dark. The recreational drinking and curiosity about drugs that had begun before our marriage grew into a lethal pattern of substance abuse.

Our children were born in this season, Molly in 1977, and Sam in 1980. Their beautiful existence was the only bright light for me, everything else a trauma blur.

Shortly after Sam was born, my German aunt came to visit. She stepped across the threshold of our flat on Twenty-Second and H in Sacramento with a look of disbelief. Dirty clothes covered the floor of the living room that doubled as our bedroom, dishes were piled high in the kitchen sink, the smell of stinky diapers and garbage wafted through the air, the baby was crying, the toddler was running around half clothed. She declared in her blunt way, "Your mother didn't raise you to live like this!" Of course, she had no idea what was going on in our lives. She lived in another town, and I didn't see her very often. She was alarmed for good reason. But I'd just had a baby and I was drowning. With our lives crumbling around us, keeping order of any sort, making and enjoying food together—it all slipped away in the chaos of our living.

Within two months of our baby boy's birth, Chuck and I were separated. What is food at a time like that but mere survival? My sister would feed us. We went for Mexican food at Luis's. I read books on child development, but nothing else. And though I didn't know it was prayer, I was praying the most basic prayer of all: *Help.*

My husband once wrote a lyric, "Time is a gift of love and grace. Without time there'd be no time to change. Time to be tried, humbled and broken. Time to hear the word of love spoken." He wrote these words in his early thirties, on the other side of what I've just described, but all the way through our lives, I've found it to be true. When things are profoundly bleak, you don't know what help may be coming, how God's Spirit is moving.

During our five months of separation, the bottom fell completely out. There was no place lower to go. And then came a glimpse of something genuine—a word, a tone of voice, a conversation. There was hope. We got back together and moved into a house I was planning to rent with a friend. With a few false starts for each of us, we began programs of recovery through Alcoholics Anonymous and Al-Anon. There was nothing quick or painless about it, but as the months added up in the sixth year of our marriage, we grew healthier. Signs of hope and new life trickled in. Those who knew us could see it reflected in our family life. By this time our children were three and a half and nearly one.

In this first year of healing, I started paying attention to food again. We had fun planting a vegetable garden and hosting our first Easter gathering. I began learning the discipline of keeping food in the house and meals on the table. I was still very much a novice when it came to making a home, but as my eyes opened to the needs around me, I started to think it mattered.

Chuck and I didn't talk about how to divide the labor. There was so much to take care of that we just dove in. I learned the bookkeeping for our self-employment, cleaned the house from week to week, sewed curtains for the bedroom windows, and planted flowers in the front yard. When Chuck called from the studio to ask if he could bring a buddy home at dinnertime, we had food to share. I saw the world of cooking open before me and grew intensely interested. We lived very close to Corti Brothers, Sacramento's legendary grocery store and wine merchant. They had the freshest and best of everything, and shopping there was pure inspiration. I also perked up at the way people around me were doing things. I noticed simple things, like the way a friend made French toast. She added vanilla and cinnamon to the egg batter—small touches, but ones I'd never thought of. And she used pure maple syrup: a revelation!

The kids and I made friends with a strange and delightful neighbor, an older woman whose given name was Ida, but who was known as Happy. Happy concocted some odd meals in her kitchen; however, she made one thing I loved—cheese cookies. The taste resembled the spicy goodness of carrot cake, with a savory hint from the cheddar cheese. I wrote the recipe down on an index card and added it to the xeroxed recipes my mom sent from time to time.

In 1982, in the weeks surrounding our seventh wedding anniversary in May, the spiritual awakening prompted by our recovery groups blossomed into a full-blown conversion to Christianity. In response to the gospel-bearing message of a saxophone player, Chuck and I came, one after the other, into new life.

It was April when my husband made a declaration and posed a question, one that threw me into a stomach-churning upheaval. He'd become a Christian, a follower of Jesus. What did I think of that? he asked. I didn't know what to make of it, but my first inclination was to pack up the kids and leave. We'd already been through so much. I was afraid and wondered if our family could survive a religious fanatic. I'd been to church off and on growing up and had never heard anyone talk like that. What did this language mean?

In high school, there were kids known as Jesus freaks, but they were off in the distance, not in my circle. I vaguely associated them with a cult. What did I know?

For our anniversary weekend, my sister Paula took the kids. Chuck and I spent the days and nights moving about in freedom, going to matinees, riding horses at a stable, and talking over meals in restaurants. The topic of Christianity threaded through our conversations. He'd been studying. Praying. He talked. I listened. I changed the subject. It came around again.

Days went by. There was a pinprick in my armor, a tiny bit of light seeping in. Questions rose to the surface that I didn't know I had. I wondered why the Bible has authority. What makes it unique? Why should I trust it?

As these things go, I just happened to find a book lying around that Chuck had borrowed. *Reasons Skeptics Should Consider Christianity*. I thumbed through the pages and had my first encounter with the world of apologetics—the work of scholars who spend their lives studying the reliability of the Scriptures through history, archaeology, reason.

One day while I was running errands in downtown Sacramento, I noticed a Bible bookstore out of the corner of my eye. I'd never seen it before, but I was drawn like a magnet. I pulled over and parked on the street. On the crowded shelf inside was a book titled *Is the Bible Sexist?* As if the spine were lit up with twinkly lights, I saw it: my next question exactly. At home, I read just enough to wonder if the Bible told a much bigger story than I'd ever known. With the coming of Jesus, freedom and dignity came to women and men both—the freedom to serve one another humbly in love. As Dorothy Sayers tells it in her small gem of a book *Are Women Human?*:

Perhaps it is no wonder that the women were first at the Cradle and last at the Cross. They had never known a man like this Man—there never has been such another. A prophet and teacher who never nagged at them, never flattered or coaxed or patronized; who never made arch jokes about them, never treated them either as "The women, God help us!" or "The ladies, God bless them!"; who rebuked without querulousness and praised without condescension; who took their questions and arguments seriously; who never mapped out their sphere for them, never urged them to be feminine or jeered at them for being female; who had no axe to grind and no uneasy male dignity to defend; who took them as he found them and was completely unself-conscious. There is no act, no sermon, no parable in the whole Gospel that borrows its pungency from female perversity; nobody could possibly guess from the words and deeds of Jesus that there was anything "funny" about woman's nature.[1]

I began reading the gospel of John and encountered the living Jesus, "The words I have spoken to you—they are full of the Spirit and life" (6:63). We visited the saxophone player's church a couple of times. I sat on the sidelines during Communion, but I was watching and listening, taking it all in, affected by their love. The Word of God, the Spirit of God, the people of God, all working together to draw me in. I resonate with Bono in his memoir, *Surrender*, "The Bible held me rapt. The words stepped off the page and followed me home."[2]

I couldn't turn back from any of these things and pretend ignorance. On one particular night, I prayed out loud with my husband by my side and our children asleep in the next room. It was my turn to join the ancient chain of people of faith and move into the arms of grace.

I have always counted that night in May as my conversion to Christianity. I wonder if God thinks of it the same way. Wasn't Christ's love expressed to me in my grandmother's kitchen, my aunt's concern, my mother's perseverance in caring for her children when her own trauma was unnamed and untreated?

But there is no denying the moment, or series of moments, when you turn to God and begin to follow. When I woke up the next morning, everything was the same and everything was different. I began to sit in a frayed, gray hand-me-down rocker with an open Bible, hungry for understanding and transformation.

We quickly got involved in the life of our new church, and I saw something I hadn't quite seen before: a whole community of people who took care of each other. In this lifestyle of caring, cooking was important. The folks in our new church opened their homes for Bible studies and provided refreshments. They took meals to people in the congregation who needed them: families with new babies, households experiencing illness or grief. My cooking repertoire expanded as I joined this work. I tried new recipes and became sensitive to the unique food needs of the people we served. I learned to consider health status and age, kids or no kids, and the kinds of situations that precipitated the need for food. All of these things would affect the menu. I also began thinking about combinations of flavor, texture, and color when I designed a meal meant to nourish body and soul.

One of the most life-giving authors I discovered in those early days was Edith Schaeffer. Fireworks went off in my brain when I read her books. Edith saw family life and caring for other people as an artwork. Through her insights I came to understand that the details of caring for human life are the playground of creativity, the place where our choices are significant in communicating love. Her language captured my imagination, and I began to long for good stories in our household, to value the work that might bring them about. Throughout her writing was a strong thread: a biblical understanding that human beings are made in the image of an Artist, the Creator of all things seen and unseen. As image-bearers, we have the capacity to imagine and create in all of life for the good of our household, our neighborhood, our city, our planet. The implications are huge for any vocation or sphere of life.

But in the context of caring for a family, along with the hospitality work to which Chuck and I were slowly being called, these implications were game-changing. These truths became foundational to all our future work. And when I thought of creating our family culture, receiving others into our lives and home, creating traditions and celebrations, and meeting people's needs for comfort, deep fellowship, and aesthetic pleasure, food seemed to figure in everywhere.

As our children grew, gathering at the table became increasingly important. Because of my husband's musical vocation, which meant long hours in the studio or weeks on the road, we were intentional about having dinner together as often as possible.

It was hard work to make it happen. Sometimes I would start a meal—chop something, marinate something—pick up the kids from school, come home, do a little more preparation, load them in the car again for baseball practice or music lessons, run home to prep some more, pick them up again, and finalize the dinner when I was home for good. It sounds crazy now! So much work for thirty minutes around the table? And still the mess to clean up after?

This is the way I remember it. One: Our budget was small and cooking helped get us through. Two: I was in a season of experimenting, trying recipes, caring for my family, but also accumulating skill, knowledge, and experience. In essence, I was training for a work I could not yet see or know. In just a few years my life would fill to the brim with houseguests and gatherings, and I would need to feed people. I would *want* to feed them. Three: I'm a big believer in the family table. Within the limitations of our imperfect life, I gave it a good try.

Whether we had a pizza delivered or I made a complicated meal, those dinners were a golden time for conversation among the four of us, a time set apart to nurture our family relationships. As rushed as they might be, it was our time to hear about each other's days, tell whatever stories were waiting to be told, and pay attention to each other, without distraction. If there were dinner guests, our table fellowship was blessed by the addition of other people's stories.

Coinciding with an increasing need to cook was my growing interest in the creative world of the culinary arts. In the mid-1980s, I came upon my first Alice Waters cookbook. The kids and I visited our friend Kathi Riley Smith, a chef then working in San Francisco and the surrounding Bay Area. We ate delectable cinnamon croissants on the beach, and in the evening, Kathi cooked a simple meal using fresh herbs, handmade pasta from a local grocery, chicken cooked to perfection, and the best produce available. I went to bed that night with the *Chez Panisse Pasta, Pizza, & Calzone* cookbook as my nighttime reading. I encountered foods I'd never heard of and cooking terms I didn't know. I was intrigued by the delicious-sounding recipes, captured by Kathi's inspiring cooking life, and curious about all the cookbooks that lined her shelves. I was eager to learn more.

I began collecting cookbooks through a book-of-the-month club. *The Classic Italian Cookbook* by Marcella Hazan was the first to arrive in the mail. I read it like a textbook, starting at the beginning and working my way through, trying recipes along the way. In the next years I accumulated a growing library of cookbooks, food magazines, and recipes written on scraps of paper. All of these recipes became my tools, the inspiration I turned to each week as I made menus and grocery lists to feed our family and our growing table of guests.

COOKING AS VOCATION

In 1989, we moved our family from California to Tennessee. Within a year of living in Nashville, we bought the old country church that became the Art House, and eventually our family home. From that point forward, cooking became even more important. Caring for people bodily, spiritually, and vocationally became a steady factor in our work.

Hospitality was always a central theme in our Art House life and feeding people an essential part of everything. It was necessary in taking care of people's physical need for sustenance, but also in providing tables at which to nurture relationships. Whether an artist at our dinner table, several people striking up a conversation over homemade cookies at a retreat, or a quiet, one-on-one meeting over coffee and muffins, food was the anchor and the occasion to stop and attend to one another.

I remember the winter we had several batches of houseguests with late-evening plane arrivals—in some cases, hours past dinnertime. In mulling over how to welcome our weary travelers with food that would stay warm and fresh on the stove until they arrived, I updated a recipe for vegetable basil soup from one of the first cookbooks I ever bought, Sunset's *Easy Basics for Good Cooking*. I used homemade chicken stock and fresh basil. (Note: Stock is easily made by simmering the bones of a roasted chicken in water—throw in onion, celery, and carrot if you have them. Freeze for later use.) To the vegetables I added good sausage, sliced and sautéed. With a hearty loaf of bread, this soup was the perfect answer to a late-night meal meant to nourish, nurture, and communicate that our guests were thought of in advance, cared about, and welcomed. Soup always does the trick!

In the first months of the pandemic in 2020, I was so grateful to have cooking knowledge. As I read news articles and listened to podcasts, I detected a slow wave of understanding moving through the culture. It was important to know how to cook. Those who didn't know their way around the kitchen began to learn. In fact, people baked so much there was a flour shortage!

Our daughter, Molly, gave us the beautiful gift of adding our grocery list to hers, dropping bags of food at our door until we could figure things out for ourselves. In those early days, I found that when you can't run to the grocery store all the time, you get more creative with what you have. You stretch it out, make it last, learn new skills.

Like many, I learned to bake sourdough bread with a glop of starter given to me by a friend. I didn't know it was a pandemic trend in America until I'd made it four times! When the first glorious loaf came out of the oven, Chuck and I each pulled off a chunk and used it for an online Communion service with our church. We served each other, *The body of Christ, broken for you.*

A few weeks later, we needed bread and I wanted the physical experience of working with my hands in the dough—turning and folding every thirty minutes for hours—followed by a slow rise overnight in the refrigerator.

Before baking two loaves in a very hot oven, I used what I had on hand to make a simple puree of potato-celery soup: potatoes and onions from a farm stand around the corner, the last few tender pieces of a celery stalk in the vegetable drawer, homemade chicken broth from my freezer, and a dried bay leaf. Salt and pepper to taste. Remove the bay leaf before pureeing the soup. Pour it back into the pot. Add a cup of half-and-half and heat gently. I served it with warm, buttered sourdough bread, and a fresh peach galette for dessert.

I cooked most nights that year, using as many different-colored vegetables as I could get my hands on. I hoped that "eating the rainbow" would give us healthy immune systems. And I cooked to create small moments of hospitality in a hard season. Sharing a tasty meal always brings a shot of comfort and cheer.

Learning to cook has opened the door to a more flourishing life. Through cooking, I've learned to comfort, celebrate, care for the sick, create traditions, welcome loved ones and strangers, and create environments for relationships to grow. Cooking has a power that goes beyond meeting our basic need for food. Creating good food and welcoming tables speaks to the deepest parts of our being. We are created to live artfully in daily life, to need real food to nourish our bodies, to have tables at which to belong, and to have stopping places where we can know and be known.

And as my grandmother did with me, I've passed food knowledge to my four grandchildren. I love spending time with them in the kitchen. It's a happy place where talk flows easily. When Brinsley is with me, we always cook. She is the youngest, but she is skilled. Lately, we've been baking chocolate lava cakes.

One month after Bridget turned eighteen, we made croissants together. From start to finish, including time to sleep while the dough rested, the process took twenty-six hours. On my own, I wouldn't have attempted something that complicated, but when a grandchild reaches out and says, "I want to bake with you. When are you available?" I'm there for all of it—time spent together, companioning in creation, a big memory.

Art and caring, skill and memory, comfort and nurture, faith and love—it's all intertwined.

Cooking matters because people matter. Feeding the hungry and welcoming the stranger are signposts of the Christian life. There are countless opportunities and ways to live these out, but learning to cook is a good place to start.

three

THE (CHRISTIAN) NAME GAME

To Musicians and Music Lovers

from Charlie

What does it mean to be a student and follower of Jesus? And what does it mean to be a musician? In my lifetime, these two questions remain perennial. Faithful language and clear answers are always needed. Hence this letter to my people, musicians. And to those vital to us—the music lovers, who follow and support the music we make.

For over forty years, I've watched and listened as well-meaning followers of Jesus have stumbled and fumbled over how to define Christian music. And I've watched frustrated musicians play with language, hoping to communicate that they are a Christian who is a musician and not a Christian musician. Or Christian by faith, rock by genre, and so on.

I've seen the misinformed zealots emphasize the naming of Christian *music* and *musician* as a sign and symbol of boldness in proclaiming Christ (over against those musicians accused of being "ashamed" for refusing the Christian music/musician moniker). And I've seen the savvy marketing mind leading with their branding, loudly telegraphing the message: If you're looking to buy Christian music or a Christian musician, we're selling it.

Thankfully, I've also witnessed the authenticity of musicians who follow Jesus, naming themselves as Christian musicians and humbly serving and loving the church through music (commercially monetized or not). I've also seen and heard the faithful witness of Christians using their musical gifts for the flourishing of people and planet (and never once calling it Christian).

My analysis is this: if we fail to answer the perennial questions just referenced with trustworthy, sustainable ideas and definitions, we can count on twice the confusion when the words *Christian* and *musician* are combined.

To the musician hoping to be faithful to the twin callings to Jesus and music, this can be a heart-wrenching, anxiety-producing quandary to find yourself in the middle of—for some, even an impasse, leaving you feeling stuck. Especially so when all you really want is to be found faithful. To Jesus of course. And to the music you believe you are called to create. I get it.

I confess that this mix-up about naming music *Christian* continues to pain and negatively affect me, even after all these years. How? Imagine creating improvisation-based music, or neoclassical, with the world's most outstanding musicians, giving God thanks for the good work, then hearing from a longtime listener, saying, "I'll pass. I'm waiting for your next Christian album."

It can be equally confusing to music lovers—also a diverse lot. Some of you were schooled to believe that *Christian* and *secular* are handy categories for keeping your music interests straight. Others of you have no strong need for genre and categorization. You simply love discovering music you enjoy. And there are all the positions and opinions in between, correct?

Which direction or theology is faithful and trustworthy?

I'm writing in hopes that my experience as a working musician for fifty-plus years and a Christian for over forty might offer you some clarity. I would love nothing more than to pass you the peace and freedom of Christ, relieve or prevent anxiety, and clear up confusion and misunderstanding. Let's give it a solid go, shall we?

First, here is some background information on me and a couple of stories related to the subject of the letter.

As for: *What does it mean to be a student and follower of Jesus? And what does it mean to be a musician?* I've been asking these questions in tandem since April 1982, when, at age twenty-five, the Jesus story was relayed to me afresh, and I believed. That was the first time I perceived these two questions to be intertwined. Till then, the pair generally kept their distance. Before following Christ, I was practicing a sacred/secular divide. I was placing music into two categories: Christian music and all the rest of the music in the world.

I'd been a working musician since I was a young teenager. But at twenty-five, the flurry of new faith activity, like praying, studying the Bible (with its esoteric, descriptive language like "being born again"), and meeting other people who self-identified as Christians, had me asking lots of questions. There was much to learn about being a committed student of Jesus. And how this new relationship might influence and affect my music-making.

Since early childhood, I'd been creating and sorting out artistry-type questions in one way or another. Writing stories and making music grew the deepest roots. No surprise there. My mother was a wordsmith, and my father a musician. I was also exposed to the music of the Christian church from an early age. My paternal grandparents made it their business to ferry my sister and me to church, even when my parents had no interest. My mother's youngest sister was my first guide to pop music via radio, television, and vinyl records. My dad was a jazzman. His record collection introduced me to Miles Davis, my seminal jazz influence. Though a self-taught pianist, I am a product of traditional music education. For example, when I left high school as a junior at sixteen, I had two years of music theory, played multiple instruments, and could sight-read jazz and symphonic music. I could also write pop songs, Bachian figured-bass pieces, and twelve-tone rows, imitating the composer Schoenberg.

All of this influence and education were important. What accompanied it, though, was the proverbial game-changer. Once the music was inside me, I wanted to know everything about the who, what, when, where, and why. Music history became important to me—especially everything twentieth century and related to jazz, pop, blues, soul, and rock.

I began reading everything available on my favorite musicians, how their art was imagined and created, and who and what they credited as influences, creatively and spiritually. My primary sources were books at the local library and magazines: *Rolling Stone*, *DownBeat*, and *Jazz & Pop*. The latter I read from cover to cover in the Yuba City High School library, not knowing that an associate editor and regular contributor would become a mentor very shortly.

Frank Kofsky (1935–1997) was an iconoclastic 1960s music journalist, Marxist historian, and amateur drummer influenced by Elvin Jones of the John Coltrane Quartet. Frank befriended me when I took his history class (Black Culture at Bicentennial) at Cal State, Sacramento, in the fall of 1976. The textbook was Frank's then controversial *Black Nationalism and the Revolution in Music*—which included, arguably, the most oft-quoted interview with saxophonist John Coltrane. Apart from the A grade I received from Frank, it was an undistinguished semester. Though an acolyte of sorts, I received an F in Zen Buddhism. This is something like an overly wordy Zen kōan: *If you receive an F for failing to drop a class and then leave university altogether, did the F really happen?* Either way, no satori awakening for me; sudden enlightenment was still several years down the road.

On a few occasions, I assisted Frank with research and transcription. He would let me tag along on an artist interview or to Keystone Korner, the famed San Francisco jazz club owned by Todd Barkan.

There, I heard the giants of jazz onstage and once backstage too. Frank liked to visit the musicians before and after gigs to capture quotes for his Bay Area Jazz column in the *Sacramento Bee*.

I was twenty years old. When you're that age and full of yourself, there's no space left for anything of external importance—even what you profess to love. I wish I could recall Frank's questions and the legendary tenor saxophonist Dexter Gordon's answers. That would be something.

At Keystone Korner I was exposed to the architects of modern jazz, including drummer Max Roach, pianist Andrew Hill, trumpeter Eddie Henderson (with whom I later recorded), vibraphonist Bobby Hutcherson, and, of course, the aforementioned Dexter.

At the time, I thought I was getting an up-close listen and look at iconoclastic historymakers. In reality, I was learning how to be a musician and artist in the world. I could articulate only a little back then regarding a cohesive philosophy, but the education was no less profound. Todd Barkan put it into words when he corresponded with me about the Dexter Gordon gig a few years back: "That is by far some of the greatest music ever played at that truly psychedelic jazz club, and I am so happy you were there to hear the miracle happen in person!"

Todd added a diamond quote that Dexter Gordon once said to him: "My shoes are dusty but my soul is clean." Classic.

Part of Frank's mentorship was to have me correspond with the enigmatic pianist Andrew Hill. His *Point of Departure* album with Eric Dolphy is a Blue Note Records classic (if you're not a jazz aficionado, just know this is heady stuff). I wrote to Mr. Hill requesting an interview for *Keyboard* magazine. He responded by letter: "Bring a bucket of chicken and something for the head."

I knew fried chicken but wasn't sure about "something for the head."

"Weed," Frank informed me.

Oh. "Are we going to bring some?" I naïvely asked.

Frank once put me in his column, describing me as a pianist of "no mean ability." Now, why couldn't he have just written "above average"? Pesky intellectuals. The full quote is entertaining: "Pianist Andrew Hill remarked to Chuck Ashworth (himself a piano player of no mean ability) and me, during the course of an interview late last year, 'If someone were to call me a jazz musician today, I would hit them in the mouth.'"

True enough. Andrew's conception of music was more extensive than the jazz genre. It reminds me of an anecdote the great Warner Bros. Records executive Lenny Waronker once shared with me about Prince telling Lenny, "Don't make me Black." Not Black as in ethnicity or identity, but genre, which at the time of Prince's first album would've been R&B—a genre too small for the musical calling on Prince's life.

Anyone following my occasional opinions on the phrase *Christian musician* or *Christian artist* might've noticed my intro salutation to this letter. I didn't use these word combinations. I have never referred to myself as a Christian musician or artist. As a genre of music, like Prince and his rejection of R&B, Christian music is a genre too small for what I've been called to. I believe in the combined words' concept and usefulness, though. Sincerely, I'm not being inconsistent.

I think use hinges on definition within a context. I'm not immune to using genre labels as shorthand to get at an idea or communicate succinctly (I've already done so several times in this letter). I draw the line at having genre labels define me or others as musicians (if it's not their desire, like Prince and the pianist Andrew Hill). Though unlike Mr. Hill, I promise not to punch anyone in the mouth!

I don't call myself a *Christian musician* or *artist* because of the familiar musical context where those terms have been used related to me. Namely, the context of the contemporary Christian music genre, known for years as CCM. I've been loosely connected to and later well established as a contributor to CCM. Concerning the music and the people, this is a fact for which I'm grateful. Of my half-century-plus years as a working musician, I was under contract for ten years as an artist, songwriter, producer, and record label to Sparrow Records, later EMI Christian Music Group—a self-identifying Christian and gospel music company (1989–99). This decade of work, and the receptivity of Christians to my first two solo albums (1984–86), naturally caused people to assume I considered myself a Christian musician in the context of CCM. I did not.

Because of my entire musical story, if I name myself a Christian musician, it will exclude me from participating in a whole range of music that I've been trained for and called to create.

Though I love, admire, and support all sorts of musicians and musical artists called to serve the church for a lifetime who refer to themselves as Christian musicians, this has not been my calling, exclusively.

Being known as a Christian musician alone does not reflect my theological convictions, artistry, or musical history. How and why this is true, and why it matters so much to me, is part of the journey that goes all the way back to the influence of my family, the church, and the musical world around me as a child, teenager, and young adult—including Frank's classroom and Keystone Korner.

I didn't come to view myself as an apprentice to Jesus by accident. There was, as there often is, a definitive event of "sudden enlightenment." I have a Spirit-sensitive saxophonist (Michael Butera) to thank for bringing me the good news of Jesus in 1982. It's also no accident how music has shaped me throughout my life. It's been a setup. One long unfolding plotline living those questions while receiving incremental, slow-going, living answers (with a few sudden, bright epiphanies too).

In the hope that it will be helpful to you, let's look at the plotlines in my story and see what we can learn. The influence of family, society, geography, education, and much more is never neutral in shaping us as people and musicians. When Jesus called me to himself, he already knew my story by heart.

I was raised by a working musician who later became an educator. This produced two complementary values in me. One, music was a *vocation* you were trained for to "make or earn a living" (using my dad's vernacular). To be a working musician, in and out of academia, meant gaining the skill and ability to play popular music at a dance or party (which my dad did, and I followed in his footsteps), play in the pit band of a musical, such as *The Music Man*, and perform as an instrumentalist or vocalist in a community concert of Handel's *Messiah*. As mentioned earlier, I studied music theory in high school, played instrumental soloist competitions, and performed in the marching, jazz, pep, and symphonic bands—and played trumpet, electric piano, and organ in local bands with other teenagers and adults. Here's the takeaway: I was learning to perform a wide range of music created for an equally wide range of use and enjoyment.

Next, my dad became a choir director at a Christian church, and he required that I participate. As a child, I had sung Sunday school songs and hymns familiar to the American church. Now I was reading melodies and choral compositions, singing arrangements in a choir context, conducted by my dad. This added another essential piece to our family story and my musical education. Let me update our takeaway sentence from a moment ago: I was learning to perform a wide range of music created for an equally wide range of use and enjoyment, including serving the Christian church as a vocalist.

While all of this was taking place, I was beginning to decide which music inspired me. What I wanted to play and write. Here, the range is also broad but can be distilled into two basic categories: all the music created by African Americans in my youth (e.g., blues, jazz, rock, gospel, soul, and R&B), as well as the 1970s-era singer-songwriters (e.g., James Taylor, Paul Simon, Jackson Browne, and Joni Mitchell).

This introduced two more important values or commitments that have remained in me and my music: improvisation, as the ability to extemporaneously compose on the spot, and lyrics as a narrative device to tell stories and examine the human condition—personally, socially, and spiritually. The latter is related to answering the question *What does it mean to be a student and follower of Jesus?* in a multiplicity of linguistic ways over a broad range of subjects. This work includes using various lyrical, literary, and poetic devices. As with the Bible and the teachings of Jesus, my lyrics are rhetorical, descriptive, prescriptive, implicit, and explicit. And, hopefully, literary and poetic too. They are missional and intentional, and occasionally mysterious, even to me. Often, a more precise, profound meaning is revealed to me over time.

The question *What does it mean to be a student and follower of Jesus?* is not solely answered in my lyrics or my profession and behavior. It is answered in the music too. The music witnesses through its diversity and capacious application to people, places, and spaces within culture for specific use and enjoyment, including the Christian church. The ability (gifting) to extemporaneously compose music (improvise) on the spot, where thought and intentionality are slices of seconds, is also a witness. It speaks to trusting both the gift and Giver—that the music is there inside me and available at any time.

I have said elsewhere that *the great object of living, the purpose of life on earth, is to form within us all that love values.* And by *love* I mean love's highest embodiment, Jesus. I've created music for decades by asking whom and what does Jesus love. The answer begins with this prayer from Ephesians 3:17–19: "And I pray that you, being rooted and established in love, may have power, together with all the Lord's holy people, to grasp how wide and long and high and deep is the love of Christ, and to know this love that surpasses knowledge—that you may be filled to the measure of all the fullness of God."

How wide, long, high, and deep? This certainly has to do with the quality and quantity of love. It's also about the object of Love's affection. Jesus is the agent of creation and the heir and sustainer of all things, and the object is Jesus' creativity. People, the planet, the universe, and all the vast creativity yet to be known or understood by the human family.

In my own small way, I have tried to make music as a witness to something of *all* that Jesus loves. And this is how I've approached those two initial questions in what I hope has become one seamless, congruent response. That's been my goal. It is how I have gauged faithfulness. Taking my cue from Galatians 6:10, I have treasured every moment that my music-making has accomplished this for anyone, anywhere. Especially when it has helped the fellowship of Jesus' followers worldwide to know and feel God's beauty, goodness, love, and grace more assuredly.

I know to whom my allegiance belongs. I know from where my ultimate worth comes. And I know the story in which I'm participating. I don't need to proclaim that *I'm a Christian musician*. Especially if to do so would so "genre-fy" my efforts as to limit my faithfulness. (See the letter "The Artist's Role in the World," chapter 7, for a deeper dive into this.)

As I mentioned earlier, I'm not alone here. Neither are you. The band U2 have spent fifty years trying to avoid a genre too small for their calling. So have others. After a short "born again" period of what was named *gospel* or *Christian* albums, the wily Bob Dylan said "enough" to being co-opted into the role of the current famous musician (in the 1980s) who had "come to Jesus." Again, a genre too small for his mission. The story of 1960s and '70s soul and R&B music is filled with Black artists criticized, even rejected by their churches, for straying from gospel music to record love songs. To do so was often considered apostasy.

Switchfoot, a band I signed and developed, has struggled with the name game their entire career. Like Amy Grant, how many hit pop singles do artists have to have for people to understand they're doing something more comprehensive than solely participating in the genre of Christian music? Or, in Amy's case, receiving a well-deserved Kennedy Center Honor in the arts (2022) while the media continued calling her "the queen of Christian pop"?

In case you feel you have to name yourself Christian—otherwise, you betray Jesus and your calling—please remember this: the word *Christian* is used only twice in the Bible. In the book of Acts, the writer recorded that Jesus' disciples were first called Christians in the ancient

Greek city of Antioch, what is today Antakya, Turkey. There is no historical evidence that early disciples of Jesus referred to themselves as Christians. *And Jesus did not name his followers Christians.* Instead, he most often referred to them in a familial way, using personal names, sons/daughters, brothers/sisters, and children of the living God.

This being so, in the earliest days of the church, it's likely that naming disciples as Christians came not from within but from without. The best evidence of this is in the Bible, again in Acts, when King Agrippa II of Judea asked Paul, a disciple of Jesus, "Do you think that in such a short time you can persuade me to be a Christian?" (26:28).

In the New Testament, there are many accurate names and descriptions of those who took Jesus' words and actions seriously. Especially *disciple*, meaning a student or follower. This name is very fitting since Jesus' students considered him a rabbi, or teacher, in the Jewish tradition. These student-followers of Jesus are also described as belonging to the Way. Likely because Jesus said of himself, "I am the way and the truth and the life" (John 14:6).

Disciples are also known as brothers and sisters, saints, heirs, and "the church" (meaning the gathering). All of these and more are used often throughout the Bible by actual disciples of Jesus, describing one another. You can use these today or develop your own inspired ways of communicating a complementary idea. This freedom is yours.

As a descriptor, there is nothing out of sorts with *Christian*. It does mean a follower of Christ or something like belonging to the party of Christ.

Whether you're a musician and student of Jesus or someone who loves the music and wants to lovingly support your favorite musicians, please consider my own personal conviction about the word *Christian* and its relationship to authentic faithfulness.

The authenticity and surety of my discipleship are not contingent on naming myself a Christian. There is a wide swath of freedom for how I describe myself as a disciple of Jesus. Also, there may be good reasons not to accept the name *Christian*, especially when doing so would harm the unfolding story of Jesus and his followers. This is not denial or being ashamed of my association with Jesus.

Unfortunately, many sincere people have been taught and believe that dedication to Christ means calling oneself a Christian. I understand. But it's simply not true. Does Jesus ask for fidelity in varied ways? Yes, and they are essential to know and live by. But calling oneself a Christian isn't even on his list. More to the point, please carefully consider Jesus' words in Matthew 10:33 for using or not using the name Christian. As with fidelity, there are many ways a person can deny (or "disown") Christ before an audience. None good. Rejecting the word *Christian* for Jesus-centric reasons is not one of them. Denying that you are a student-follower of Jesus when, in truth, you are. There you go. That would be it.

Dear reader, I hope this helps clarify and provide solutions for the anxiety and confusion-producing name game this has become, particularly around specific vocations like music and the arts. And that's really what we're looking at here. Dishwashers, sawmill workers, volleyball players, and orthodontists don't have this problem.

HONOR AND RESPONSIBILITY

Thank you for your patience in allowing me to lay the groundwork for the finish to come. Now we can look at a trustworthy application of the word *Christian* and the honor and responsibility of being known as a Christian or Christian musician.

If I call myself a Christian musician, both words' definitions are made trustworthy only through faithfulness. We can trust each other as authentic Christian musicians when we see and hear sustainable practices of Jesus-congruent and music-congruent daily living (never perfect, but proximate). For each practice, we are called to love and care for what Jesus loves and cares for.

Then there is the quality of how that love and care is made evident in the world: our work, our creativity—the music itself. The hopeful goal is that our professions about life in Christ will be congruent with the creativity we imagine and bring into the world. Remember, our discipleship and music is one cohesive witness made of two integrated callings. A loving and faithful Christian, unfaithful to developing musical skill and ability, doesn't make for a trustworthy Christian musician. The inverse is also true. Point made, I hope.

We define these words by our behavior, our witness. But communities of professing Christians also create their own unique definitions and prioritize particular ways of being and doing. These can be Jesus-congruent, or confusing and contradictory. Ultimately, whether the word *Christian* is of any value for human and planet flourishing is dependent on trustworthy community and theology (which I'll call *our shared thoughts on all things Christian*).

There has to be some shared agreement about what the word *Christian* means. And agreement on what sort of result we hope for if we are known by the word. Whenever shared agreement is lacking, confusion emerges, and the word *Christian* loses efficacious meaning.

As common as this outcome is, it doesn't have to be this way.

For example, I can think of a handful of friends and small communities of people with and by whom I would feel very comfortable calling myself or being called a Christian musician. I'd be honored.

What the what? How and why?

I would know and trust we have shared meanings and definitions because we've actually talked about such things. I would be confident that we have more in common than not as to what being a student of Jesus and music means. We would know something significant about each other's stories—again, because we would have been in active, storytelling communion with one another. In my case, they would know my eclectic musical background; training; the ability to compose nearly every form of American music, European-derived classical, and some forms of African music. And they would know I have served the church worldwide by writing and producing songs that *brothers and sisters* have used and enjoyed for many purposes, including fellowship and musical worship. They would know that everything I've been trying to do as a musician for the past four decades is about loving all that Jesus loves, bearing witness through music and daily living (in my own small way).

In short, they would bear trustworthy witness to who I actually am as a disciple and musician, and I would reciprocate. This is to know and be known. The heart cry of every human being. This kind of setting, one of shared meaning and mission, is where words make good.

Now let's look at Christian music as a genre. There are reasons to identify music as *Christian* as a convenience. For example, a skilled Christian composer and lyricist is a solid choice if you want a new hymn created around a particular topic or set of Scripture verses. In a close Christian community, though, using the word *Christian* is usually unnecessary. The musically skilled people in the community are choosing or creating music to serve the fellowship using their abilities, discernment, and aesthetics—in cooperation with others within the like-minded cohort. As all music-making ought to be, it is prayerful, loving work. The question is always this: How do we love the gathering of Jesus' people through music? The Lenten season may have a unique answer, as will new songs needed for primary-school children.

Where genre, and the functional naming of things *Christian*, really comes into play is with music companies that are developing songwriters, producers, recording artists, and worship leaders to create music for the church as a service and a business. My son-in-law, Mark, is an executive for one of these companies. Their customer is looking for Christian music (as their larger community and company define it). The company's focus is on loving the church through music by identifying and resourcing musical people who have the same mission. This sort of Christian naming, in general, is functional, benign use. If you visit the hardware store and ask for lawn-care products, you don't want to be directed to paint, right?

The Christian music genre is also one slice of a demographic that large entertainment corporations attempt to cater to (where most of my personal experience is). Here I associate with the good people and artists I've been privileged to work with, the music we've made, and the enthusiastic listeners. I do not associate with the genre exclusively. If the pop, Americana, or jazz communities attempted to exclusively associate me with their branding work (e.g., "He's an Americana producer"), I would reject it as well. As much as I may respect the people involved in all the music I love making, I'm against anything systemic that truncates, or actually prohibits, my ability to live into and faithfully answer: *What does it mean to be a student and follower of Jesus? And what does it mean to be a musician?*

Readers, several things are true at once. I can see that naming things *Christian* is a benefit to fellow Christians. I can love and support people who choose to name their work or themselves *Christian*. And I can ask that I not be called a Christian musician exclusively, because of my particular calling as a student of Jesus and creator of music.

If you live and work within a trustworthy community that makes naming yourself or being named a Christian musician sensical, faithful, and beautifully efficacious—please rest in the freedom to use and accept the name. If you feel and think that a community truncates your musical calling with its language and branding, then by all means, exercise your freedom and reject it.

Always choose the fullness of faithfulness to Jesus and music first. That's all he's asking of you as a disciple and a musician. That way, you live up to the Name above all names and bear good witness to the art that finds its genesis in the Name. It's the only name game in town. The only one worth playing.

four

A LEGACY OF SHELTER

To Those Who Long to Love
a Place and Use It Well

from Andi

Most people who go to the trouble and expense of buying a second home want to be near a lake, the mountains, or the beach. That's why it was strange for us to buy a place in our California hometown—the one we had moved *away* from. Yuba City has none of those things, though a two-hour car ride west will take you to San Francisco, and a two-hour drive east, to Lake Tahoe and the Sierra Nevada mountain range. But on its own, Yuba City is mostly a place you return to if you have family there. Which we do. Lots of them.

It's rare for anyone to leave the area. We are the exception, moving first to Sacramento and then to Nashville, Tennessee, followed several years later by my sister-in-law and brother-in-law and their children. A migration of sorts, but in the opposite direction of all our grandparents, who came west from somewhere else: Louisiana, Oklahoma, Iowa, Missouri, New Mexico. As families do, we multiplied in Nashville, and our West Coast people multiplied. So, in 2005, when buying real estate in California seemed like a good investment, the real motivation was relational. We wanted to spend more time with our family, especially my aging mother-in-law, and see our West Coast friends too.

With our laptops, as well as music technologies for Chuck, we were able to keep daytime work hours and be with our people in the evenings and weekends. We did quiet work in a quiet house. I was in a master's degree program with a hybrid mixture of course offerings, some on campus, most online, so I could listen to lectures, write papers, and take tests wherever I happened to be. My husband was beginning to write his family history and part of the draw to California was to feel the dirt under his feet and see the Sutter Buttes from the front door.

If we had a speaking engagement or something music related anywhere on the west side of the country, we went to Yuba City before or after. Until the 2008 financial crisis eventually led to the loss of the home in 2012, we made a lot of cross-country trips.

That house on Heidi Way brought gifts I wasn't expecting. The Yuba City family used it for large birthday and anniversary gatherings and helped maintain it in our absence. Our kids and their families had a place to stay when they were in town. A few artist friends stayed a night or two with their bands as they traveled up and down the state. But mostly, it was just the two of us. The house gave us something we needed. Peace. Rest. Play. The balm of California blue-sky mornings. We named it Casa de Paz, House of Peace.

Since Chuck and I had ridden bikes all over town when we were kids, he bought two one-speed cruisers to keep in the garage. It was such a fun surprise to find them! In Yuba City, the terrain is flat and there are bike lanes everywhere. We usually arrived exhausted from our Nashville life, so we hopped on those bikes three or four times a day, basking in the warmth of the sun, and feeling the weight of the world drop off our shoulders.

On one of our visits, we toured the important landmarks of our youth—Chuck's grammar school, his neighborhood on Carmelita

Drive, the parking lot at Yuba City High School where we'd met in marching band rehearsals our freshman year, and, finally, to the site of my grandparents' house, where they'd lived until their deaths in the last half of the '70s.

I'd driven by that house many times on previous visits, but this time it was different. Because of the bikes, my senses were more engaged. As we rode on the same cracked and lumpy sidewalks I'd walked on as a girl, I felt like I was entering another time zone. We stopped at the corner of B Street and Fruitvale, got off our bikes, and looked over the back fence. The house was very different, mostly tattered and run-down. Minor efforts at repair had served only to strip the home of its former character. The whole place had been painted a dull beige. No more cheery 1940s green trim around the doors and windows of a white house.

But certain key things were still there and my memories filled in what wasn't: the tree in the backyard where our rope swing had hung, the corner where my grandparents had made a sandbox from an old tire, and the shed where my grandfather had repaired and restored golf clubs. The shed had also held a large freezer full of ice cream, ice milk, and sherbet, staples, along with homemade cookies, in the dessert life of my grandparents' home. Whenever I was there for dinner, my grandma walked me on the short path from the screened-in back porch to the shed to choose a flavor. We ate together at her small kitchen table, talking of everything and nothing. Whether by myself or with a sister, I was content and happy in my grandparents' care.

Many decades later that old house still holds my best memories of growing up. My grandfather loved us and we knew it, but it was my grandmother's ordinary, consistent, and welcoming care that had an impact on us for life.

My sister Paula has a photograph of the two of us tucked into the wood-framed bed we slept in when we spent the night. Just looking at that picture conjures feelings of safety and my grandmother's nighttime scent of Listerine and bath powder.

The places of our lives are a strong trigger for memories. As I stood at that fence so many years later, I breathed a silent, spontaneous prayer of overwhelming gratitude, *Thank you, Lord, for giving me the shelter of this place and these people.*

Shelter is a strong and beautiful word. It gets in your head and rolls around in your imagination. What can it mean to create a place that shelters people, to be a safe person for others? While I knew nothing of it as a girl, I would grow up to have a calling that built on the hospitality my grandparents gave to me. It would involve a lot more people but keep the essence of what I found at their house. And it would be given inside the great imperfection of an unfinished life and all we had yet to learn.

Imperfections and all, I am still convinced that part of the good work we can do in this life is to give shelter to each other, reflecting in small ways who and what God is for us, and learning what it means to be a hospitable people in the uniqueness of our individual stories. Hospitality to family, friends, and strangers is a way of life portrayed in the Bible and given as the best, most God-honoring way to live. Instead of hoarding, we're called to share—to share kindness and respect, resources, dinner tables, expertise, comfort, companionship, cups of coffee, beds, and couches. The realization that every good thing we have is a gift creates gratitude, and a view of hospitality as a giving way of life, rather than only an occasional evening of "entertaining."

In the life of our family, hospitality has been what Eugene Peterson called "a long obedience in the same direction." I continue to learn about it, often in hindsight. In many ways a hospitable lifestyle can become second nature, but it's never easily lived out for anyone. There is no perfect balance in this life; instead, there is grace in the tension.

Sometimes I wonder what it would have been like to be older and more mature when I got married. If I knew going in what the years would require, would it have made a difference? Would I have been better, knowing what I had chosen?

But do any of us really know? We hold hands and step into a

future we can only guess at or hope for, a future that becomes flesh-and-bone reality as we live.

One thing has become clear over time. If we had not moved from the small town where we grew up, and eventually left California, we wouldn't have made it to the rest of our story. There was another setting just waiting for us, a plotline yet to be revealed.

In the spring of 1989, the kids and I were having dinner with three longtime dear friends. Chuck was in Nashville recording vocals for a Margaret Becker album. When I picked up the phone in our Sacramento kitchen to hear his voice on the other end of the line, I knew something serious was at hand. He used the phrases *magical, fairy tale, a great place to raise a family* to describe what he was seeing. Before he left, there had been some chatter about moving to Nashville, but I thought it would pass. It didn't. He was already meeting with music business folks, looking at houses, and checking out schools.

Nashville in May is particularly beautiful. The hillsides are lush with green from the spring rains, flower gardens are blooming all over the city, and once the temperature climbs and joins with humidity, fireflies appear. But beauty wasn't the only draw. There was something deeper happening.

For one thing, we were struggling financially in Sacramento and Nashville promised plenty of work for a talented record producer. It was also an easier place from which to tour. Chuck was ready to go where we needed to go. His mind was spinning with the possibilities.

Me? I don't leave anywhere easily. Deep and connected relationships keep me tethered. Our children were old enough to be sad about leaving but too young to really process being so far from their grandparents.

I'm convinced that our great adventure the previous summer prepared us for change. Along with Jimmy and Michelle Abegg and their three girls, we had camped across America and back. Four adults and five children in one large van, pulling a tiny U-Haul trailer stuffed with camping gear, food, books, guitars, art supplies, and boxes of T-shirts and cassette tapes to sell at concerts. Chuck and Jimmy were two-thirds of a musical trio, the Charlie Peacock Group, and they had gigs at music festivals outside of Boston and Chicago. Michelle and I usually stayed behind and held down the fort while our husbands traveled the world, but this time we made a collective decision to turn a series of summer gigs into a cross-country exploration with our families.

After the majesty of the Grand Canyon and the beautiful colors of New Mexico, we woke up one morning next to a cow pasture just outside Hydro, Oklahoma. We walked down Beale Street in Memphis; saw horse and buggies in Amish country in Pennsylvania, the museums of Washington, DC, and Niagara Falls in upstate New York. On the way home, we took a detour through Blakesburg, Iowa, to hunt for Jimmy's great-grandparents' house and continued west via Colorado and Arches National Park in Utah. We pulled into our driveway in Sacramento after six weeks on the road, the children's artwork taped to the ceiling of the van, large bags of dirty laundry, and nine exhausted travelers, full of stories and ready for the comforts of home. But the experience had changed us. We knew there was life outside the boundaries of California.

For a woman like me who craves stability, it's telling how quickly I felt a spark of excitement about moving to Nashville one year later. I reasoned that God seemed to be closing doors in Sacramento and opening new ones in Tennessee. By July, we sold the first house we'd ever owned, packed a moving truck, and, with the help of a friend, drove it across the country, this time in four days.

Our first year in Nashville, I alternated between extreme homesickness and feeling curiously interested in this new city. Summer thunderstorms that poured rain under only one cloud. Air that was thick with insects. Kids who said *Yes, sir* and *No, ma'am*. And food. When California folks came to visit, we took them to Herbert's Barbeque for pulled pork and sweet corn bread, and the storied Loveless Cafe for fried chicken and biscuits. The local cuisine and waitresses who called everyone "honey" were part of Nashville's charm.

After moving from an apartment into a neighborhood of newly

constructed homes, I knocked on doors and introduced myself, handing over plates of freshly baked muffins or cookies with our names and phone number taped to the covering. Cold-calling on strangers was not in my comfort zone. I'd never done it before. But I sensed that if I wanted to live in a welcoming neighborhood, I'd have to help create it. Something about the South seemed to draw me out and make me willing to risk knocking.

I developed friendships with some of the women, walked with them through hard patches, helped give baby showers, and enjoyed the occasional neighborhood backyard barbeque with other families. When Chuck was gone, the kids and I had phone numbers and people to call on if we needed them, and that was a comfort. I was seeking the shelter of other people, putting down roots, planting trees in the backyard.

And then a sudden twist in the story. In September 1990, only a year and two months after we'd moved to Nashville, a topic appears out of nowhere in my journal, accompanied by a scripture:

> We looked inside the old church home today. Chuck and I both had intense emotional reactions to it. Is it the future home of the Art House and the future home of the Ashworths as well? We both feel yes to the first, and uncertain but leaning toward the second. There's so much that seems perfectly fitted to us—the large kitchen and walk-in pantry, the bookshelves that line the walls, the huge dining room table, the back porch, all the different rooms, the beautiful, old hardwood floor and cathedral windows. So much could happen there.
>
> Isaiah 27:2 & 3, "Sing about a fruitful vineyard: I, the LORD, watch over it; I water it continually. I guard it day and night so that no one may harm it."

Chuck had been in Europe for a summer tour. Back home, he tried to explain the ideas that had grown more vivid as he traveled. He wrote about it later in *New Way to Be Human*: "The words of Jesus to Peter in the book of John rang like timpani rolls in my skull. God was saying to me, 'If you love me, feed my sheep. Go get them, care for them and feed them. Give them a place of shelter.' That's how I began to dream of a place where young artists could gather for friendship, community, and teaching. I gave my imaginary place a name: the Art House."[1]

The old church referenced in my journal was located down the street from our neighborhood. We passed it every time we went to the grocery store or left the community of Bellevue in a northern direction. We'd always been drawn to the building, curious about what went on there and who owned it. One day as we drove past with the kids in the car, there was a For Sale sign out front. Chuck wondered out loud: "Maybe that's the Art House!"

Within days, we had an appointment and were knocking at the kitchen door. It was opened by a tall, lanky, older man named Lester Moore. His wife, Sybil, stood at the stove cooking bacon. They were friendly and quirky, Sybil with a thick Southern accent. They showed us around the place and told us a little about it. We got back in the car and burst out crying, neither one of us knowing why.

The next day we went back with Molly and Sam and our dear friend Aaron Smith. They all fell in love with it too. We stayed for an hour and a half listening to Sybil and Lester's stories of the vacant church they'd bought at an auction in 1977 and turned into their home.

After our second visit, Chuck took me through his journals, where Art House ideas and convictions lived in their formative stages. He'd even drawn a logo.

In our life together it's not unusual for Chuck to chew on big ideas for a long time before they come to the light of day in conversation with me. But I'm a processor, one who needs to have all the available information, sit with it, pray, and gradually come to know my own mind. These two styles, pray-as-you-move and pray-and-wait, are both good, born of our God-given personalities. But they also hold the tensions of our life together—my need for information and time, and Chuck living in his head, then wanting to move quickly because he had already processed.

Several factors helped me along the way of decision-making.

For most of a decade, I'd been drawn to the life and work Edith Schaeffer wrote about in her books. Edith was cofounder with her husband, Francis, of L'Abri Fellowship, which began in 1955 in their home in Switzerland and now has branches all over the world. The Schaeffers created a safe place for people to come with their honest questions and struggles about Christianity, and how it relates to all of life. *L'Abri* is the French word for shelter.

There is no mistaking that Edith's writings had a shaping effect on me, but I already knew enough about the realities of hospitality not to be completely dazzled by her stories. Still, the combination of intellectual and physical hospitality they offered was inspiring and helped me recognize what my own work might be. As Chuck and I talked and sought counsel from others, the words *care, service, hospitality, shelter,* and *teaching* were used. Those were resonating words for me. They always had been. I began to have a vision of my own for the kind of timeless, personal care that would be given if the place became our own.

After seeing the church with us and listening to us talk about it, our friend Aaron made this simple statement: "God gives us the desire to follow him into specific callings, and the faith to pursue them without knowing all the particulars." That made sense to me.

Also in the mix, I was depressed, struggling with a lot of anxiety, and lonely for my husband. Since moving to Nashville, life on the road and in the studio had never stopped for him. Art House was something we were to do as a family. That was appealing.

I was intellectually hungry. I loved reading books, studying, and writing. I loved cooking, gardening, place-making, theology, and relationships. I had no idea how those things could come together to make a whole, but that's what I brought with me.

I wanted to let Chuck pursue his dream. If it failed, I knew God would still be with us. I was inspired, my mind filling with possibilities and the excitement of a new chapter. And I was scared.

I wavered back and forth between the readiness to move ahead and waking up at 3:00 a.m. with buckets of worries pouring into my head. I was overwhelmed with the financial responsibility we were about to take on. Less than a year before, I had been praying for living expenses, a winter coat, and money to buy Christmas gifts. Chuck was worried too, but he was sure we were supposed to do it.

This is how he described it: "Lester told me he'd carry the mortgage note if I could come up with a down payment, which might as well have been a million dollars. We simply could not afford it. . . . At the same time Sparrow Records approached me about leasing some of my older recordings. I drove down to Music Row, to the first Sparrow Records office in Nashville, and met with Billy Ray Hearn. We discussed the financial part of the deal. He offered me one amount, and I countered him with a figure that matched Lester's down payment. 'All right,' Billy Ray said, 'we'll do it for that.'"[2]

On October 10, 1990, less than a month after we'd first looked at the church, we closed on the Art House. We met Sybil and Lester at a lawyer's office and signed a bunch of papers and payment schedules that would keep us extremely dependent on God for a long time to come.

I held Sybil's hand while the tears flowed down her face. They were selling the place because it was too much for them to care for in their older age, not because they didn't love it. She was emotionally tied to the house and leaving was extremely painful. The old church was powerful in that way. To become a part of its ongoing history meant being pulled into the emotional center of its being.

Wendell Berry's novel *Hannah Coulter* is one of my favorite books of all time. It's a wise and beautiful story about Hannah, a woman twice widowed who's looking back on her life and sorting through her memories. Along the way she comes to tell of the house and land where she lived and farmed with her second husband, Nathan: "Sometimes

I imagine another young couple, strong and full of desire, coming quietly into this old house that will be empty again of all that is of any use, and will be stale and silent and dingy with dust, and they will see it shining before them as Nathan and I saw it fifty-two years ago. And I say, 'Welcome! Love each other. Love this place and use it well. Bless your hearts.'"[3]

When I read this passage, it caught my breath. It made sense of Sybil and Lester's story, and ours, and, much later, Nathan and Cassie Tasker's, who would move into the church after we left. We were all stewarding a building and its land, loved and used well since 1912, when it was formally dedicated as the site of the Belleview Methodist Episcopal Church South. In 1969, the church moved to a new and larger building down the street and became the Bellevue United Methodist Church. There were some in-between years when the building was used for a variety of purposes other than church services. But eventually it became "stale and silent and dingy with dust," with holes in the floor and ceiling. In 1977, Sybil and Lester came along and bought the church for their son to live in, but when he lost interest, they moved in and began the long process of restoration, transforming the church building into their home. Sybil said that when her son lived in the place, she would spend time there listening to classical music and drinking in the peace. That's when she began to harbor a secret love affair with the old church.

She told a reporter of a local newspaper, "People call me and ask if they can use the house for their parties and such. I just can't say no. This place is so big I just have to share it." They hosted weddings, charitable events, parties, and picnics.

Sybil's love affair with the house was passed on to us. After the Moores moved out, the Art House sat empty for a time. No quick HGTV-style flip, the church and God's vision for it took time. I'd drive by and toss out a prayer, or stop in and sit on a chair that had been left behind, asking God, "What is this place supposed to be? What will we do here? Please guide us."

Through Chuck's musical travels, he had become acquainted with two young men, Douglas McKelvey and Nick Barré, who'd been roommates in college and were newly graduated. They were sharp, funny, and passionate about art, music, literature, and film. And they would end up joining us in Nashville. Nick became our first Art House director. We had no furniture yet, only borrowed brown metal folding chairs, and no money to pay him, so for room and board Nick began in the way of a young bachelor serving Jesus. With grace and good humor, he made a cozy bedroom out of a large storage closet in the second-floor loft and helped us get going.

With the support of Nick and Doug, and many other friends, the public life of the Art House began in the summer of 1991. It started with a Bible study taught by Nashville pastor Scotty Smith. The study provided a weekly staple and a theological centerpiece for everything else we did, like gathering around topics such as "Cultivating the Mind of an Artist," "Obstacles to Creative Living," "Transcendence in Film," and "The Artful Life."

When the chairs filled up in the chapel space, folks sat on the floor in the hallway, in the loft area, and the room next to the kitchen. A wide variety of people and age groups came, including out-of-towners who were passing through Nashville. But the largest weekly audience were twentysomethings and college students from Vanderbilt and Belmont Universities. For many it was their first serious study of the Bible. The Art House became a place where students or newcomers to Nashville forged lasting relationships.

As soon as we bought the place, I had an immediate sense of the mood and environment I wanted to create. It was inspired by my grandmother's house, the novels of Elizabeth Goudge, and my own intuition—the guidance of the Spirit. It was as much about a feeling as it was a look.

My friend Maggie and I scoured secondhand stores looking for old, sturdy dishes. Molly and Sam chipped in, and we made dozens of homemade cookies every week. It made us happy to see people lingering and talking over drinks and dessert. We served ice-cold lemonade in the summer and hot apple cider, coffee, and tea when the seasons changed. I found a huge old pot that had already seen a lot of life, and filled it with apple juice, ground cinnamon and cloves, and sliced oranges. Hot cider was a staple whenever we had a fall or winter gathering in all the years to come. The scent filled the kitchen and welcomed people into the house.

We continued to live in our house down the street for three years, then finally made the decision to make the Art House our home. The financial burden of paying for two places, along with keeping up with the maintenance, was wearing us down. Moving was necessary, but hard. This would be our eighth move in the sixteen years since Molly was born. I was invested in our neighborhood and loved the nearness of people I'd come to know. I didn't want to leave it. Chuck and I argued for months. We went to a counselor for some clarity. I could see a glimpse of possibility at the Art House, but mainly I saw a big, empty church building that filled with folding chairs and people several times a week, and drop-in visitors the rest of the time.

Earlier that year, with a loan from Chuck's parents, we'd had the detached garage torn down and built a recording studio and office. Musicians and engineers came day and night to make records. The property was a place for art-making, business, and public gatherings, but it wasn't a family home, and I had become emotionally detached from it. I couldn't truly love the place or put my personal stamp on it without living there, but the thought of pulling up stakes again was overwhelming. I was confused and hopeful at the same time, not knowing whether Chuck was pushing or God was calling, or how both might be tangled up together.

I made pros-and-cons lists. One of the pros I wrote down was that a move to the Art House would fulfill Dan Allender's definition of work based on 1 Peter 4:10—the basis by which we live out the talents God has given us for the larger good of others. I would have the ability to develop and use my gifts in a more thorough and ongoing way. I knew the Art House was a means of grace in people's lives already. I couldn't deny that God was using the place, even though I realized only a fraction of it. In my heart, I couldn't walk away.

As they say, the rest is history. We began to love our place up close: renovating, planting, hosting, making music and making food and making family. Now it was personal. People came into our kitchen, gathered in our living room, stayed in our bedrooms. We had our first epic New Year's Eve party with friends, visiting family, and a new young band from San Diego called Switchfoot. There were grandmas and teenagers, everyone dancing the Electric Slide to Janet Jackson's song "Escapade," Sam shooting off fireworks at midnight.

Just a few months after moving, we woke up in the middle of the night to the sound of tree branches crashing and power lines snapping. It was an ice storm. By morning, most of the city had lost power and the schools had all closed. Our house was one of the few in Bellevue that still had electricity. It became a refuge for friends, and friends of friends, who had no light or heat.

The first night as we gathered in the kitchen sharing pizza, there was a knock at the door. We opened it to find a desperate-looking man standing there awkwardly holding an ice pack to the front of his sweatpants. Chuck recognized him right away, a fellow musician named Rick. Rick didn't know it was our house he'd come to. He simply saw the lights on and thought he was knocking at the door of a church. He had his family in the car—his wife, a seven-day-old baby, two very young boys, and his parents. The reason for the ice pack? Rick was four hours out of a vasectomy. This family needed help! They joined our pizza party and slept on mattresses on the floor in the big room.

Shelter. Sharing. Story after story.

Oh, dear friend, it is not easy to find the path ahead. We can only say yes to the moment we're in, looking to Christ, the Good Shepherd who leads us in love. The puzzle pieces of our callings drop into place day by day. Sometimes we are overwhelmed. Other times overjoyed.

In the beginning, it was extremely hard for me to adjust to life in a home that had so many different purposes. We kept trying to find our way. Over time, the Art House became a true home. We stayed for over two decades.

By God's enabling and over many years, thousands of people came through our doors for gatherings or one-on-one conversation. There were meals, weddings, retreats, speakers, music, and holiday celebrations, all worthy of their own stories. I could drop some famous names to spice things up, but as Chuck once said, and I fully agree, every person was famous to us. In the midst of it all we made a home, lived our marriage, finished raising our children, and welcomed our grandchildren. All along, we sought to create a shelter that would mean something to our own family but also make room for others. Like my grandmother did in her house, and Wendell Berry does through his own life and the lives of his fictional characters, we tried to love our place and use it well.

At its essence, shelter is about people and place. Or as my husband always teaches, all the stories of our lives are about God, people, and place. It's people who bring a place to life and make the intentional choices to create a shelter from whatever resources they have. And it's God who moves among us, welcoming us to himself, and asking us in turn to be a welcoming people. Eugene Peterson translates Romans 12:13 as "be inventive in hospitality" (MSG). I love that. There is no cookie-cutter way of doing things and no household that has the same callings to live out. In addition, there is no year in anyone's life when the needs we come across will be the same as the year before.

It was normal for us to have a steady stream of house and dinner guests, people working with us or passing through town on some business or another who needed a place to stay. Hotel prices are prohibitive and, for some people weary of life on the road, just plain unwanted. Sheltering travelers is a practice as old as the human race, as necessary today as it's been throughout history. I was constantly learning.

Thanks to its elevation on a small hill, our house was one of the few in our neighborhood that survived the Nashville flood in 2010.

The needs all around us were overwhelming, and it was difficult to know where to start in offering help. We prayed for guidance and had a full house that first week but subsequently became a part of providing a home base for our eighty-two-year-old friend Betty. She lost most of her belongings, and like hundreds of others affected by the flood, her home had to be gutted and rebuilt. The needs in Nashville after the flood were astronomical, but in the midst of the devastation a beautiful thing happened. People showed up in droves all over the city to give help. Friends and strangers dragged ruined furniture and other soggy items to the street, brought sandwiches and water to the workers, and tore down moldy drywall. Others opened their homes and offered shelter to those who'd lost their own. We were not the only people to host our friend Betty. Other friends offered their homes too, and she moved among us, never without people who loved her during a terribly difficult and disorienting time.

This picture from our Nashville community is a reminder to me of the way God has called us to live. No one can do it all. Each person has a role to play, gifts to share, and the particular needs of place and communities to consider and respond to. And everyone needs cycles of rest and refreshment.

At the end of that summer, I wrote a note for myself in the guestbook *Houseguest sabbatical from August to the end of December 2010*. In order to concentrate on other aspects of Art House hospitality, we needed a break from that particular form. A home that's known for its welcome is like a runaway train. It's hard to get off. But there is also a deeper truth, which many people share: when you work from home in any capacity, whether paid or unpaid, the lines are blurry about when to start and stop, when to rest and play.

I always longed for mentors to help us with guidelines for all the complexity. In my constant search for a sustainable vocation, I knew it was good and right before God to be human. Having houseguests one after another for long periods of time is taxing. My creeping mental and physical exhaustion was telling me something. In all our years of practicing hospitality, I learned that in order to continue offering it, it was wise to rest when weariness set in. We learn as we go. May you have the wisdom to know when to open your doors and when to close them for a season. And may your life, dear reader, be the church that offers welcome to those who knock on your door.

five

ON BECOMING A
LIGHT IN THE CITY

To the Concerned Citizen

from Charlie

City-making has been going on for a very long time. Remember the story of Babel? And there's Jericho, a city still on the map today, thought to be 9,600 years old. The influence of the deep past remains. To this day, we create cities using the grid plan developed by the ancient Greeks.

There's a powerful, cosmic relationship between us and the cities we build. Of all the creative work humanity has teased out of the earth, none compares to the city. We shape the city of our hopes and dreams, and then the city turns and shapes our dreams afresh and renews our hope. Or it doesn't. There is no neutrality. On the whole, a city is either improving or deteriorating. Each of us determines the outcome.

If the genesis of a city takes aspiration and planning, the flourishing of the city requires a diversity of unrelenting hopes and dreams for the betterment of all its citizens. If there's a problem with cities, and there are many, the betterment of every dweller is the first to go. Whenever cities are afflicted with great trouble, you will see a disappearing middle class, the absence of affordable housing (or housing altogether), failure to care for the poor, the homeless, immigrants, or veterans. You will see a lack of preparation in order to survive catastrophic storms, and the failure to provide green space, funding for the arts, or infrastructure upkeep and improvements. The list is long. City trouble comes in many shapes and sizes and always seems to affect the most vulnerable the worst.

So what's a citizen to do? We vote, right? We speak out. We pay taxes. But we actually do much more than this. Some of it is intentional. Some of it we never give any thought to. There's no neutrality in citizenship. I see the creation of cities the same as creating anything. I'm contributing either to the light or to the darkness. With this stark contrast, I choose light. I choose to be a light in the city, and I hope you do as well.

City-making is small, individual work before it's the building of stadiums, schools, roadways, or incentives to attract business. To be sure, it's definitely about all of that. But in a city the size of Nashville, where I live, it's also about the millions of personal choices and stories that shape the imagination and creativity of our city. City-making is the work of the people before it's the work of the politician or planner. Every citizen is empowered to produce good for the betterment of the city, no matter how small or large their contribution. Every citizen can be a bright light for good. City government aside for a moment, we all govern and are not without power.

One of my grandchildren, Robert, was once a superhero with great strength and powers (I would argue this is still true). As a little boy, if his powers collapsed inward and drifted from love, his parents would gently remind him: "Robert, use your powers for good." I imagine this encouragement applies to all people in all places, superheroes or not.

When Robert attended an elementary school down the street from his home, he and his father, Mark, began their day with what they called a *walkabout*. They would walk and talk their way to Robert's kindergarten class a half mile down the road. At bedtime, Mommy (my daughter, Molly) joined them to talk to God about matters of mutual concern (prayer), and then Robert and Daddy ended their day with a *talkabout*—a subject of Robert's choosing, or a summary of the hours and action that preceded bedtime.

This way of being with a child is a simple recipe for goodness. One all of us can benefit from. Walk together. Talk together. Pray together. Have a sense of the day's events and how they make up a life. Allow for curiosity. Be a good listener. Get some sleep and rise to do it all again. Not in sameness but as a framework for intention and improvisation leading to human flourishing.

Using powers for good is at the heart of the local-global narrative I hold to. But it's certainly not exclusive to my people or place (say, followers of Jesus in Nashville, Tennessee). Nevertheless, we use some time-tested language to get at this idea, such as "Love your neighbor as yourself" and "Do good and share with others." This language of loving reciprocity threads its way through history and nearly every expression of religion and philosophy. I think it's safe to say that using one's powers for good is the better part of the human mission.

Over the past four decades, I've heard and been party to much discussion and debate about engaging culture or entering into the culture-making fray. I think that *entering* and *engaging* is fundamentally flawed language. Culture is made everywhere and engaged by everyone. If you're breathing, you're making and engaging culture. No need to "enter." As my friend David Dark says, borrowing from an old television ad, "You're soaking in it."

The helpful neighborhood-loving, city-making questions are these: What kind of culture am I making? Is my "soaking in it" imaginatively and creatively intentional? Am I concerned with the quality of my making in all its forms? Which way do I lean—maker or taker? And for me, as someone who professes to be a student of Jesus, I ask:

Is my cultural witness (word, work, and play) seamless and congruent with Christ's renewal mission? For clarity's sake, this is a question I ask knowing full well my weaknesses and failures, past, present, and yet to come. Perfect is off the table. My approach is to always work with an awareness of grace. As the wise philosopher Dallas Willard once wrote: "Grace is not opposed to effort. It is opposed to earning."[1]

Not sure what the sum of your powers are? Take an inventory. Some I would list include: music and art creation, teaching, the care of my immediate neighborhood, my contribution to the upbringing of young citizens like my children and grandchildren, and caring for those in need. What are yours?

Make a plan for how to use your unique passions, talents, skills, and resources for the betterment of the city—to let your light shine. It doesn't have to be perfect or complete. Which is okay, because it won't be. An inventory of powers and a plan to use them never hurts though. It's a beginning. My family and I have seven practices we trust and do our best to embody—to the degree that they are possible and within our power. I'll pass them on with the same exhortation to do as you have opportunity:

1. Be city-centric in your making and spending.

   All of us in the collective family are grateful to have our work used and enjoyed locally. Since most of our music, art, and writing go beyond our city and around the globe, whenever I have opportunity, I identify myself as a Nashville artist or Nashville music producer. I want people to know where the songs they enjoy originate. With internet shopping just a click away, it is difficult not to avail ourselves of it. Even so, Andi is intentional in buying her books at our neighborhood bookstore—novelist Ann Patchett's Parnassus Books—and when possible, she uses a local pharmacy rather than one of the chains.

2. Support your locally sourced nonprofits.

   One of our great joys is to support nonprofits doing work

in the lives of children around the world. The need is great. Yet, even in the best cities, the needs may be different, but no less dire or challenging. Some of the nonprofits we support and work with are concerned with: family crises, homelessness, the unique challenges to families due to music touring, food insecurity, clean water, hospice care, and the care of immigrants to our city. Make a note of those near you. Ask friends and family for recommendations. Get involved. A pair of willing hands cleaning or praying is just as essential as giving money. Any help given, though, is good help.

3. Promote belief in a lifelong education and the synergy of the city and its arts and institutions.

I believe that the bigger your world in heart and mind, the better you are as a citizen at the local level. Higher education is just the beginning. There is always something good to be learned. Expand your heart and mind by becoming a lifelong learner. Be curious. Ask lots of questions. There is nothing more inspiring than meeting someone in their eighties who is still taking risks and eager to learn. In many ways, being a student of life, for life, helps with aging, keeping the brain (and often the body) nimble. Finally, support the arts in your city and those individuals and institutions that serve the arts. It is a fact that if you want to find a great city to live in, look for one where the arts are a flourishing part of the city's identity.

4. Contribute to the spiritual life of the city.

I have a saying: "There is no common good without sharing good in common." If spiritual life isn't spilling out of the church and overflowing into our cities and all that we have in common, then the church needs help. And there's no spiritual help to be had without the Spirit of God. The mission of the Spirit is to make you and me a unique kind of citizen, to live a good life that is good because it speaks, it tells the story of someone faithfully following Jesus. What will this look like?

Here's a short list of goodness: grace, humility, empathy, peace, hope, mercy, justice, generosity, kindness, patience, and love for God and neighbor.

Contributing to the spiritual life of a city takes many forms, including the obvious like supporting your local Christian gathering and bearing witness to the grace of God in Christ. The majority of our contribution, though, will be everywhere *but* the church. This is when and where that short list is meant to be embodied. Your contribution to the spiritual life of the city will never be greater than the story your life tells. A life story is big enough to hold the simplicity of praying for your city, and the complexity of having two hundred employees that you pay far more than minimum wage (generosity), who have health-care options, including paid maternity and adoption leave (empathy, kindness, neighbor love). Pray, use your imagination, and get creative.

5. Stay in deliberate, lifelong contact (friendship) with young people just beginning their life paths as well as people further down the road.

You were once the next generation, and now it is your turn to support those coming up. You are less a teacher/mentor/sage than a student/listener. Be humble, helpful, and not a hindrance. Think less about any generational disagreements and more about the humanity you share. These simple ways of being and doing make for a better city, for a healthy, generationally integrated citizenry. If our hearts, minds, and arms are wide open, the benefit of friendship with youth is youthfulness. Why is this a goal? A defining characteristic of a healthy young person is hope for a better future and the willingness to do the work to ensure it. A way of being, profitable at any age.

Younger readers, I hope you caught that last bit. We are counting on you for a better future and confident you'll do the work set before you to ensure it. As future oriented as you must be, don't forget the past, don't fail to study it or respect it, though. Often, clues to a good way forward are embedded in the wisdom of the past. Be assured that some of your elders knew exactly what to do regarding a city-making problem, but the timing wasn't right and the support wasn't there. Take that wisdom and bring it into the present and future.

6. Raise your children to take their place as helpful, productive citizens.

Simply put, this sort of citizen cares about people and planet, and the city where they live. Care always means stewardship and service, imagination and creativity. Parenting is the noble task of citizen-making. Parent the child to become the adult you will one day meet. This requires living a good story in their presence, passing on to them the best information about the most important things, placing a higher premium on empathy and imagination than performance, lots of prayer and patience, and, very often, learning to live with delayed satisfaction. In some instances, there is so much out of your control that hope for fruit of this kind of nurture feels improbable, even impossible. In all things we acknowledge our brokenness, the challenges of life, and for all of it there is much grace. Ultimately, parenting is love embodied for every circumstance, not governed by the clock.

7. Cultivate the place and people entrusted to you.

In the same way that farmers and gardeners cultivate patches of land to produce food and beauty, cultivate your dwellings, businesses, and institutions to be places of inspiration and uniqueness. For any people you oversee, create an environment where good will happen. As with the other six practices, imagination and creativity play a role here. Taking an inventory of all you steward will make your mission clear. Think of where you dwell, work, and play, and where you meet with other followers of Jesus. Then ask these questions: In all of these categories, what exactly is in my care? If not in my direct care, are there ways I can contribute? Once you've pondered all of this, you can evaluate the quality (and sometimes quantity) of your care. If you are not satisfied with something, take another run at imagining something better and creating it.

I'm thinking of the most basic and simple stuff here. For example, I drive by the front of my house and realize I should fix that paint that's chipping off and plant something in the beds that will bloom for the whole season. It's tempting to wonder how in the world this makes a difference. Do the math. Multiply the action by the number of citizens. In Nashville, any good multiplied by seven hundred thousand citizens is a lot of good.

The power that personal aesthetic choices have to change the tone and hue of a city was driven home to me decades ago. I was in Poland soon after the Berlin Wall came down. Huge changes were afoot for Eastern Europe. In the city of Katowice, where we were performing, the city was dark with age, neglect, and coal soot. Yet, out on the margins where country met city, citizens were growing bright flowers and hearty vegetables. The presence of the planting served as a light for the present but also as a direction for the future. People need color and light and to touch the earth and be touched by it. Never underestimate this.

Closer to home, I love the story that musical artist Shara Nova (My Brightest Diamond) once shared about her friend and artist Erin Martinez. Both women were in Detroit to be part of the urban garden movement. Erin would dig up roses from empty lots where houses were torn down and replant the roses in a garden. That way, what was seemingly lost was found, and what someone once loved and cared for was loved and cared for again.

I want more of this kind of living and less of anything that isn't this. I want my music-making to be powerfully good. I want the food production and gardening on our property to be powerfully good. I want my problem-solving to be powerfully good. I want my fathering and grandfathering to be powerfully good. I feel a *talkabout* coming on—talking to God and people about matters of mutual concern.

I wonder, how can I—how can all of us—more intentionally imagine and create for the good of our cities, planet, and neighbors near and far?

six

WHY NO PART IS TOO SMALL TO MATTER

To Those Who Need Reminding of the Greatness of Small Things

from Andi

I have a date with myself most Saturday mornings. It starts in the kitchen with a search for the right coffee cup. Are you familiar with this ritual? After putting the coffee on or heating water in a teapot, you stand bleary-eyed in front of an open cupboard and stare. It's a lot to ask of a cup, but I'm looking for something: Inspiration. A good reminder. A feeling. A cup that's not too small or too large. I consider the white cup with the green-lettered Eudora Welty quote about writing, the yellow-handled cup with Robert's artwork, and the wine-colored mug from Strand Book Store in New York. Is it too early for a Christmas cup, I wonder? Details. This one small choice takes less than a minute, but I can't deny its tiny yet meaningful place in the day.

With coffee in hand, I round the corner to my office and grab a black fine-point pen, the small weekly planner that lies open on my desk, and my journal. A cadmium-green artist journal with cream-colored, unlined pages of the perfect thickness. If it's warm outside and the garden is blooming, I go to the porch. But in the cold months, I plug in the twinkle lights on the fireplace mantel and settle into an old leather chair in the living room.

While my head clears from sleep, I look around the room to orient myself. I see book stacks on the dusty coffee table, a vase of orange tulips, art on the walls. My eyes pause at the glass doors leading to the garden. For a split second, I think about getting out the Windex and tackling the dirty windowpanes. That thought leaves as quickly as it came. I will not be distracted.

I open my journal to the next empty page and write the date at the top, then wait for a moment to feel the quiet pleasure of anticipation. When I'm ready, I begin to write the details of the week that just passed, consulting the planner to help me remember. I document, reflect, process.

As I write, words flow easily from brain to hand to pen to paper. The blank page is a refuge. I need it like oxygen—the contemplation, the slowing down, the recording of time. It is helpful, medicinal. When the weeks feel like a blur, I can see they're not. Each day has definition. Each week has its own story.

This habit has a history. When I was a little girl growing up in California, I kept a purple diary with bits of childish news scattered across the pages. I wrote down my love for the Beatles, piano-lesson day, eating a turkey sandwich at Sam's Hof Brau. In high school, the drama increased as our class learned the practice of journaling from our favorite English teacher, Margie Toft. She taught us to put our teenaged thoughts and lives into spiral-bound notebooks. It was helpful, mostly embarrassing to read now, but still a window into an era. At the age of twenty-eight, I started a grown-up diary. It was January 1984.

I began writing exactly five days after coming home to Sacramento from my mother's funeral in Yuba City. It was late at night. The kids were asleep. Chuck was in the studio working on his album *Lie Down in the Grass.* And I was alone with my grief. I found some typing paper and a pen, pulled up a chair at the dining room table, and wrote the entire story of my mom's cancer, recording things exactly as they were, with a special focus on her final week at home. I wrote about the fear in her eyes, the loving presence of the hospice nurse, my sister Paula and me baking chocolate chip cookies in the middle of the night as an act of normalcy. When our mother stopped breathing, I sat cross-legged next to her on the bed, holding her hand and leaning down to smell her hair, aching to keep her scent etched in my memory.

I wrote down these details narrative-style, the way you do when something has just been experienced and can be documented with the most accuracy.

A few days later, I bought a small, lavender cloth-covered diary. When I could name it, I wrote down my sorrow, a little here, a little there. Along with the grief, I made short entries about daily life. There was no regularity to the writing, just bits and pieces whenever I had a moment. The title of a book I was reading or playing Tinkertoys on the floor with Sam. When that first diary was full, I bought another, and another.

To date I have fifty-nine of these books lined up on two shelves in my office, along with the one I'm currently writing in that sits on my desk. I think of them as a series of handwritten history books that capture the minutiae and momentous, the usual and unusual from every week since 1984.

I was inspired to keep these written accounts of daily life after inheriting some of my grandmother's diaries when she died. As a mother of young children, I was drawn to the idea of chronicling the parts of our day-to-day life that would otherwise be lost and forgotten with time. Reading my grandmother's words helped me see there was quiet beauty in the ordinary and routine, and that it was worth capturing the days on paper if you wanted to see what your life was made of. When the details were written down and not allowed to disappear with each day's sunset, they were given a place of importance. You could see the necessity of all the bits and pieces in the creation of a whole, and how fidelity in the small things enabled life to continue, and even to flourish.

My grandmother was a teacher, but when she married my widowed grandfather in her forties and took on the care of his two children, she became a seamstress who worked from home. Many of her diary pages contain only the fragment of a sentence—"Sewed and listened to baseball game." Other pages report cleaning the house, having friends over for dinner, canning peaches, meeting with clients, teaching vacation Bible school, ironing, paying bills, running errands. And as my grandchildren will one day find their stories in my pages, I find myself in hers. September 3, 1964, "Andrea here again today. We made doll clothes." By keeping track of her daily life and relationships, my grandma gave a cheerful dignity to all the particulars.

As I reflected on her diaries from the perspective of adulthood, I could see that all of these ordinary activities were the magic that made being with her the safest and best part of my childhood. The small things added up to become provision for her family, church, and community.

When I began keeping my own records, I held on to the sacred place of the quotidian as my grandmother had. I wrote down everything—all that it took for my musical husband and me to make a living and a life, and to grow into our callings as God revealed them with the years.

As my journals filled with the details of my children growing up and their children growing up, years of writing, hosting, and friendships—the words on the page gave me eyes to see the significance of the smaller things that are always present.

Sure, there are high points, nameable moments of climax—but most of my daily life still takes place in the in-between. I sit for hours at my computer laboring over words and sentences. I live in grocery stores and farmers' markets, at the stove and the kitchen sink. I pull weeds in the garden, fold laundry, get the oil changed in the car.

If I once thought the landscape of older age would be more spacious, I've learned it's not. There is still so much to care for: insurance calls with long waits, more medical appointments, endless stacks of paperwork to handle. I deal with the most immediate and make piles that come right up to the edge of my writing space. I get frustrated. Why is there so much complexity at a time when simplicity would be helpful?

On my better days, I remember to be thankful that we *have* insurance and health care, but I confess I will never be good at handling the business end of anything. Writing things down helps my perspective. Even the paperwork has its proper context.

As I watch my grown children and friends putting together their own puzzle of moving pieces, I see paid and unpaid work all mixed up in a big, beautiful stew of provision for their families and communities. We need reminders at every stage of life that our bits and pieces have meaning. At one time or another, we will struggle with feeling invisible and weary and lonely in the work. It's hard to do the small things over and over and believe they are part of what God is doing in the world, especially when the work feels slow and ordinary.

To all of you I say, I see what you're doing and it's hard. I'm cheering you on. I'm proud of you. Don't forget to take walks, enjoy conversations, and watch the flowers bloom!

In June 2022, I bought dahlia tubers at a local nursery and planted them in my garden. The packaging promised a gorgeous array of pinks and corals with tinges of yellow and white. I was excited. Giddy even. The plants emerged slowly. They grew strong and tall. I visited them morning, noon, and evening, like a liturgy. I watched for flower buds, coaxing them into being with dreams of their existence. When the dahlias finally started to bloom in early August, I welcomed them as royalty. From August to November I cut the flowers every few days and placed them in vases around our house. They were intensely beautiful. A gift. In some strange but real way, the dahlias were a comfort, an expectation of joy that did not disappoint. A small thing. A valuable thing. A cup of cold water.

We are a chronic-pain household. Back pain for me, an intractable headache for Chuck. On the days I see my husband in his worst suffering, I scan my brain for small comforts to offer. "May I get you a cold washcloth for your forehead? How about a drink of water?" "Shall I lie quietly here beside you, or would you rather be alone?" "Maybe some tapioca pudding for tonight?"

In February 2012, I sat proudly in the audience as my husband joined the Civil Wars in receiving one of their two Grammy Awards for *Barton Hollow*, a recording he produced. For at least a week afterward, there were congratulatory posts on social media every day. And then we came home to Nashville from Los Angeles, and Chuck settled back into the studio, taking up his work on another project—sitting at the computer editing recordings for hours on end, emailing musicians, juggling schedules, dealing with cancellations, running out to rent a violin. For every finished recording there are a thousand small tasks behind it.

So it goes for all of us—a thousand small tasks. I get weary of the things that endlessly repeat. Messes to clean up. Meals to think about. But there are also days when I'm glad to get up from the writing desk to tend to the routines of cooking dinner or doing the laundry. I find relief in turning from the stress of a deadline to a different kind of labor, one that involves moving my body, and where the results are seen or felt immediately, even if they're only temporary. The need to provide food, clothing, and shelter is a perpetual part of the work of being human. And it's often only when these things are neglected, or absent, or when we're sick and can't tend to them that we're able to see how important they are.

In one way or another, the care of human life is at the heart of all vocation. Love of God and love of neighbor is the fuel. I find perspective for the less glorious and more behind-the-scenes aspects of what this can mean when I'm centered in the reality of Colossians 3:23–24: "Whatever you do, work at it with all your heart. . . . It is the Lord Christ you are serving." As Os Guinness wrote in *The Call*, "Living before the Audience of One transforms all our endeavors."[1]

I remember the week we had two of our grandchildren at the Art House more than a decade ago. They came to work every day with our son, who was working with his father in the studio. I loved that the summer schedule made it possible for them to be with us, and I wanted to be present as much as possible. In order to immerse with the kids while staying true to other commitments, I got up early each morning to work on an essay before they arrived and stayed up late responding to emails after they went home. Most everything else was done with the kids' involvement.

We didn't do anything grand or incredibly exciting, but with kids, routine days, imagination, and the fellowship of doing things together almost always result in a good time. We made one trip to the farm stand for fresh vegetables and fruits, swam twice at the YMCA, and gave one whole day to cooking a meal for dear friends who'd just had a baby. To help out, my then six-year-old grandson, Alfie, stood on a chair and peeled the peaches for a peach-blackberry crisp. On other days we played UNO and made pancakes. They did art projects, played in a kids' pool in our yard, spent time in the studio with their dad and grandfather, and played with their aunt who took a day off to be with them.

At the time, it was impossible to know if something small and fleeting would become something large and more permanent, or to ascribe a hierarchy of meaning to the week's activities. How could I say what was most important? Was it the work of making music that would bless the world and pay the bills? Was it writing an essay that might play a small but fruitful part in other people's lives? Was it cooking a meal and delivering it to friends in need, or seizing the moment to spend time with grandchildren and make memories from the stuff of ordinary life?

When I finally sat down to write about that week in my journal, all of it got equal billing. Diarists and poets put the ordinary under a microscope and call attention to its beauty. In the work of love there is no part too small to matter and no part so great that it trumps everything else. These are the things God has called us to do, and in all of these vocational spheres—as grandparents, friends, music-makers, writers, and more—we are working out what it means to love our neighbor as we love ourselves in our little corner of the world.

seven

THE ARTIST'S ROLE
IN THE WORLD

To the Artist and the Artful

from Charlie

There is no subject I've investigated more than the artistic vocation and how it is that we discover and fulfill our individual artistic callings. Still, I rarely ponder, *Hmm, now what is the artist's role again?* Or *How did I come to know what I know about being an artist?* Only because it's like breathing. It wasn't always that way. My understanding of artistry was assembled over time through many experiences and influences. And I'm not done learning. This is a lifetime work.

Much of what I do know is the natural outcome of my experience doing the work of an artist—learning on the job and living the autodidact life. I've combined this way of knowing (self-learning) with a pinch of the traditional (books mostly—some formal schooling), sitting at the feet of a few wise art theologians and cultural apologists, and the incalculable education that comes from living and working among artists for a lifetime.

But you also need to know this: I see my life and work as inextricably entwined with the person and teachings of Jesus. He is my spiritual and artistic Teacher. His creativity is my school. What I believe about the artist's role in the world is anchored in this confession. The disciple life has resulted in the artistic life, which is my witness.

What I'm about to share will last you a lifetime. This includes three essential pearls and sparks that lit my intellect, emotions, and imagination and gave me a Jesus- and art-centric foundation robust enough to sustain artistry and discipleship. I'm calling them *pearls* and *sparks* for a reason. There is the apparent allusion to the pearl of great price from Matthew 13, but also the fact that a mollusk must mature before it can even begin creating a pearl—then it can be years of development before the pearl is complete. On the other hand, a spark is immediate and more like an epiphany or Malcolm Gladwell's blink thesis.[1] And, of course, one spark can light a bright and long-lasting fire. Here's to all of this for you as you read.

First, a story to set the stage.

On November 10, 2022, the organization Wedgwood Circle celebrated its fifteenth anniversary in Nashville. A small group of friends, including Mark Rodgers, Mako Fujimura, Dave Kiersznowski, and Steve Garber, founded Wedgwood to unite arts creators with investors and philanthropists. As a cofounder, I was eager to celebrate this ad hoc collection of harmonious folks and our history together. In those fifteen years, Wedgwood had raised over $20 million in capital, funding hundreds of artists and projects, including the bands Sleeping at Last and Johnnyswim; Martin Scorsese's film *Silence*; a theater production of *Babette's Feast*; musician Jon Batiste; and my own daughter-in-law, singer-songwriter Ruby Amanfu.

I agreed to assemble the "family band" for a legacy concert. It wasn't until the final note that I realized how succinctly the night had embodied my several-decades-old dream for the role of the artist in the world, and for music specifically, diving into the "ocean of possibilities"—a phrase I'd used twenty years earlier in my book *At the Crossroads*.

I began the concert with my parents' influence, weaving Mom's wordsmithing into the introduction. Then I created a mash-up of Dad's favorite song, "Fly Me to the Moon," and my own, "In the Light." We projected photos of Dad with trumpet in hand and my great-grandfather Baggett with his fiddle to show the generational continuity of calling. Next was my son, Sam. He performed his Grammy- and Oscar-nominated song "Speak Now" from the film *One Night in Miami*. Sam introduced his wife and songwriting partner, Ruby Amanfu, and we honored her for the remarkable achievement of receiving nominations for the Grammy Song of the Year in 2020 and 2022. First, with "Hard Place" by H.E.R. (cowritten with Sam), and then with "A Beautiful Noise" by Alicia Keys and Brandi Carlile.

Ruby created an especially poignant moment in the set when she sang "Every Step," a song written the year before with her uncle, the late Dr. Paul Kwami, director of the Fisk Jubilee Singers for thirty-plus years. The *New York Times* said this about Uncle Paul in its 2022 obituary: "He took the storied Black musical group to new heights, including its first Grammy win and a National Medal of Arts."

I asked Jac Thompson and Grant Parker, two of the best students from my tenure as director of the School of Music at Lipscomb University, to perform. They sang Jac's "Pull My Chute." As I'd hoped, they received generous funding from a patron immediately following the concert.

I brought my son-in-law, Mark Nicholas, to the stage for an unexpected finish. Mark, a VP at Integrity Music, is a talent-development expert. Mark brought up Dwan Hill, one of his Grammy-winning songwriter/producers. Dwan and friends had recently begun a pop-up project called the Choir Room—a no-frills, ad hoc gathering of people and songs. Folders of music are passed out to the attendees (think hundreds), and you're asked to declare if you're a soprano, alto, tenor, or bass (SATB). A song is chosen, and Dwan sings the individual SATB parts for reference. Got it? I hope so because the party is about to catch fire!

Dwan and six friends led all of us Wedgwood attendees in a taste of the Choir Room. It was electric. Imagine the intensity of a NASCAR pit stop, the joy of a Christmas candlelight service, and the surprise of receiving a wholly undeserved gift—all bound together in Dwan's humble yet ecstatic direction. That's the Choir Room. We closed with Edwin Hawkins's classic "Oh Happy Day." And it was.

Before the concert, author/pastor Russ Ramsey offered a beautifully insightful presentation. Russ spoke from his book *Rembrandt Is in the Wind: Learning to Love Art Through the Eyes of Faith.* His words on Van Gogh were profound. Decades earlier, right out of university, Russ came to Nashville and labored alongside us as a writer and Art House worker.

In one family and a few friends, for a couple of hours on a Thursday night in Nashville, a tiny slice of a grand vision of diverse artistic faithfulness was fulfilled: understanding the role of the artist in the world, creating the songs the whole world sings, and lovingly caring for the church through music, literature, and art. This has always been my dream and life calling.

This brings me to the first pearl and spark: The artist's role in the world involves God's people being artistic for everyone, everywhere, and in everything inspired and directed by the law of love. Memorize this, and don't ever lose it. I must emphasize how important this good news is. There is not one role for the artist in the world, Christian or otherwise. There are incalculable roles expressed in equally innumerable ways of being artistic.

Let's review the concert again and identify some of these roles and ways. A limerick was read, and elders were honored. A classic standard, "Fly Me to the Moon" (a song made famous by thousands of singers), was sung. The life and work of Van Gogh were remembered with great insight. A ubiquitous song from the band dc Talk (most associated with Christian rock and rap) was performed, and the audience sang along. Current Oscar- and Grammy-nominated Top 40 pop hits rang out. Ruby performed the song to honor her uncle's legacy and point afresh to the Fisk Jubilee Singers—a Christ-centric, African American vocal group so crucial to Nashville we would not be known as Music City without them. A new female indie recording artist debuted a single. The audience, repurposed as an ad hoc gospel choir, sang an English hymn from 1755, reinvented by a Black choir director from Berkeley, California, in 1967, becoming an international Top 40 hit in 1968. We sang the vocal arrangement of the song used in the film *Sister Act 2*, a musical comedy from 1993. Whew! And all of this was accompanied by photography and artwork I had assembled as a visual backdrop.

Was this a Christian concert? Culturally, as most folks understand it, no. In the truest sense of the Jesus mission and the calling to be God's artistic people for everyone, everywhere, in everything? Yes, indeed! In a small way, it showed something of the story of artistic people at work and play in the world and pointed to what Jesus loves (if only in part).

The artist's role is communally revealed and embodied in acts of individual and group faithfulness. It is not genre specific per se, not even "Christian" in how the word is used to denote an audience, genre, or market share. Instead, it is vast in scope, multigenerational, multifunctional, and chronically resistant to being nailed down to a one-and-done definition. And rightfully so. Why? Because the definition is never complete and constantly evolving.

As long as there are people, place, circumstance, the fuel of love, and the newness Jesus inaugurated still unfolding, you can count on an evolving definition of the artist's role in the world and the ways we express our artistic callings. The definition builds new trustworthy information upon proven, already existing bedrock—just like the gospel's good news. Good story begets good story, and we are enriched by all of it, as are generations to come.

What is fantastically beautiful about all of this is that right now you are receiving an invitation to join in, to get in on the action. The calling is to live out the artist's role in the present and future (imagining new dreams for the role as people, place, and circumstances evolve).

At the center of this vast calling is equally immense freedom, what Romans 8:21 calls *the glorious freedom of the children of God.* Without it, you cannot fulfill your calling. True God-imparted freedom is essential to God-honoring artistry.

Let's call this fact our second pearl and spark, shall we? And let's remember that our freedom in Christ is assured and complete but only manifest, or blatant and potent, to the degree that we functionally trust God's grace and love. At the heart of the glorious freedom of the children of God is the knowledge that *grace is sufficient for every sin and error* and that *love is so supreme and unconditional that there's nothing you can do to make God love you more or love you less.*

This is astonishingly great news!

As with the first pearl and spark, memorize the second too. With reverence for God, you can put away fear and false ideas of religious and artistic performance and simply be where you are or go where you are sent. *There are faithful, graceful, well-loved students of Jesus living out this immeasurable freedom to be artistic everywhere, in everything, for everyone. So come on!*

This brings me back to my phrase "ocean of possibilities." The smaller our view of the artist's role, the less faithful our participation will be. Instead of an ocean of possibilities, we'll end up with a twelve-ounce glass of the possible and predictable. I dare say, dear readers, not only is this not the way of the artist; it is hardly the way of the student of Jesus. A good reminder of what Jesus is up to and what we've been invited to participate in is found in Revelation 21:5, where he who sits on the throne said, "I am making everything new!" All things. Redemption is happening, and love is on the move. Your freedom and invitation to participate in the redemption of all things artistic are assured. Create from this peace and confidence.

Artists still have individual callings that are uniquely focused. That is, they are called to see one of the many possibilities and be faithful to it. While some folks are called to several artistic pursuits (myself included), a unique focus is the norm.

A musician might be called to serve the church for a lifetime. This is an essential, noble calling. Another directly serves the church occasionally but primarily tours the world as a violin soloist with symphonies. Another musician creates music for social media posts. Yet another plays trumpet in the Marine Band, gigging at the White House. There are thousands of unique examples of musicians exercising their freedom and playing their individual roles. No one artist can be everywhere, in all things, for all people, at all times. That enormous task is the collective role of the beloved global gathering of artists, in every generation, across time.

Even though you may have a specific artistic calling, I hope you will fully grasp and enthusiastically promote this: *we can be consistently inspired and grateful that an ocean of possibilities for artmaking exists to faithfully participate in.* Tell this story at every opportunity, and dream as big and unique as you desire. Pray for direction and inspiration, and let the love of God and neighbor be your guide. Whether the artistic work is ever named *Christian* is not the point, any more than it concerns Mount Everest, bullfrogs, clouds, and black holes. It is all of God, or none of it is. Decide where you stand.

Our individual responsibility is never to limit our free imagination except as the law of love may require. Our neighbors deserve the same opportunity for the love of God and neighbor to have a positive effect on them personally and on their artistic choices. This is freedom and the way of love. There's no need for any artistic law enforcement. What we need in the Christian church are well-versed, positive, encouraging people who promote the kind of free, love-centric artmaking I'm writing about. Which naturally includes all the contributions artists make to the functioning of the church in the world.

One of the consistent errors of the Christian church over the centuries has been to require the arts to speak in didactic, declarative, or representational ways only. This sort of art takes the form of (1) art plus Bible verses, (2) art that depicts Bible events and characters, and (3) art used in worship (predominantly music).

The problem is not having explicit art forms for the church, such as poetry, symbols, icons, woodwork, stained glass, hymns, and a timeless painting, such as the *Last Supper*. On the contrary, the artistic traditions of the church are a wealth of spiritual riches.

The perennial error is failing to encourage and support artists to care for the church *and* to faithfully till other sections of the earthly field—to play other essential parts of the artist's role in the world. The reasons for this are many and beyond the scope of this letter. I can touch on an ongoing dilemma, though. Christian people often have difficulty understanding or identifying art that is faithful and congruent with the Bible, the larger unfolding story of history in general, and even Jesus specifically. As a result, they either don't know or lack confidence in discerning who and what to name as beneficial to people and the planet generally and to the church specifically.

Here's an example of this from my own life.

Many years ago, I wrote a song that was a contemporary version of the Song of Solomon, part of a whole album examining marriage, titled *Love Life*. The album was released by Sparrow Records, a well-respected, self-identifying Christian company. Because of this one song, echoing lyrical verses from the Old Testament, an entire chain of stores sent their product back to the label with a note to the president: "When Charlie Peacock starts making Christian music again, we'll start selling it."

This and Amy Grant's album *Heart in Motion*, which I also participated in ("Every Heartbeat"), ignited a debate within the gospel music community about what was and wasn't Christian music. The brouhaha was a perfect storm of an earnest desire to be faithful to God, biblical and art illiteracy, marketing and branding agendas, and that hoary old chestnut *sacred and secular*.

Is there a time and place to name things as Christian? Yes, when the definition is *all that is congruent with, and faithful to, the person, teaching, and work of Jesus Christ*. Living under a description like this comes with responsibility, though—specifically, spending your entire life studying, experiencing, and learning to discern what is and isn't congruent. And even then, every honest person has to admit their faithfulness will always be proximate, and there will always be more to learn and plenty of correction to receive.

How can we be assured we're participating in creative work that is congruent and that will bear good fruit? Excellent question.

The answer begins with God's creativity, known and yet to be discovered. This is your model and inspiration for creating. Look at the radical diversity of creation. Be astonished at what continues to be discovered. Learn to recognize the potential for congruent personal choices, artistic and otherwise.

For example, in every civilization, God's creativity has inspired all sorts of new contributions to the world. It might be the structural design of a coral reef, the healing properties of a plant, or the use of a specific frequency in the sound spectrum. Creation is filled with usefulness, beauty, and tons of head-scratching mystery. We have yet to learn why so many things in creation exist. Some we declare of no practical use at all. Yet the Supreme Artist included them in the grand masterpiece that is all of creation. Ponder this and be set free.

Expand your idea of usefulness. All the work (creativity) of God speaks, teaches, inspires, and confounds. And it can simply exist, free and agenda-less, never poked, prodded, exploited, or monetized. Or, as humans have always done, we can create ways to use God's creativity for human flourishing.

You could spend your entire life creating art congruent (harmonious) with God's creativity. Some of it, like a peach tree, will turn up the applause. I love peaches. Make something congruent with the blobfish (voted the world's ugliest animal), and you'll likely hear crickets or disgust. No one gets the blobfish but the Artist who created it and a handful of open-minded fish biologists. Look at it this way: you, the artist, are in good company with the Artist. Being underappreciated and misunderstood comes with the gig.

How does the faithful artist cope if such delightful and expansive freedom can lead to critique, underappreciation, and misunderstanding?

Point your compass at God's finished revelation to humanity through Jesus, the living Word. Your Teacher, Jesus, and the mission he's invited you to participate in are everything. Jesus will guide you in living out the artist's role in the world. Focus your attention on all that Jesus inaugurated and invited humanity to participate in. Not exactly sure what that is? In short, it is *everything*. You are called to be a loving and gifted participant at every turn in the Jesus mission of *new humanity and new heavens and earth.*

The library of sixty-six books we call the Bible is a help—useful for *teaching, rebuking, correcting, and training in righteousness.* See yourself as stepping into this grand narrative, playing your role, in your time.

Some caution and context are needed, though. The Bible is filled with many types of communication and literature that speak to us even today. Be an openhearted, responsible listener/reader. There is forthtelling (this is), foretelling (this will be), and history (this was). There is text that is *explicit*, *implicit*, *descriptive*, and *prescriptive* (note: learn to tell the difference). There are proverbs, songs, acrostics, poetry, and much more (again, study to understand the differences—knowing the kind of literature you're reading and its function is essential). Nevertheless, whenever and however the will and ways of God for humanity are communicated through the Bible, you can be confident the Spirit of God is bringing help and guidance.

The obvious relayed, here's another cosmic fact: the will and ways of Jesus are not always communicated through words.

Beauty has a deep reach and a loud voice. Embodied justice rivals Pavarotti's volume. Righteous anger whispers and shouts. Whenever the will and way of Jesus are accomplished, the Spirit is with you. Trust that the Spirit has unlimited ways of communicating and touching the whole person, which are equally efficacious as words. This is how much of God's creativity and our artwork speak and connect. Let them have their unique language and visceral affection, even if you don't always understand what's happening (yet).

Never let go of the foundational truth that love is the highest and best way of knowing and discerning (as taught by Jesus). In his famous summary of the Law, Jesus showed us that an epistemology of love is to be front-loaded into all human experience, including the arts. Even reading the Bible and applying verses to life. Jesus' command to love first is the portal that everything must pass through and return through. Paul was in agreement: *without love, all is nothing.*

Remember, the Spirit of God is presiding over everything, imparting to you wisdom, comfort, knowledge, ability, and unique, right-on-time insights and inspiration. And, most remarkably, your Spirit-led imagination will coax into view artistic creativity for your particular moment in history (everything you need to play your role with confidence and humility). Trust this with your whole person: *with great patience, the Spirit moves us along through life, incrementally gifting us with wisdom and insight and the ability to embody something of the mystery of God at work in the cosmos.*

How huge is this? It is the stuff of stardust. Celebrate, give thanks, and embody your enthusiasm in your art and life.

Our ocean of possibilities creates an environment of vast freedom—personally and, as a result, artistically. Remember, freedom is the grace-filled vibe in the room. Breathe it in. That other feeling? It is God's unconditional love for you. New ambition and mission? That's the calling to be a Jesus-inspired artist everywhere, in everything, for everyone. Answer the call with every part of yourself and your life. Dear reader, rise and fear no more.

Do you sense a nudge to care for the artistic needs of those who gather in the name of Jesus? Carry on. Want to spend a season creating work that represents your understanding of beauty? By all means, do it. Angry about the misuse of power by political leaders? Artfully tell the story and create contrast between the darkness of humanity and the light we are capable of. Curious to know what the excellent imagination untethered might produce? Use the richness of your human faculties and your freedom in Christ, and bring into the world something wholly unique. If I pick up on it, I'll jump out of my skin excitedly. And I'll talk to God about it, saying, "Thank you for the good creativity this artist has added to the world."

I could riff on this unlimited mission for hours. From the moment forty-plus years ago when I received the first hint that an "ocean of possibilities" was the calling, I've been dreaming and working to embody it. I have not been alone. Andi has been right in sync with me. Many friends and more share this calling, including the painter Mako Fujimura; poet-journalist Steve Turner; singer-songwriter Sara Groves; drummer Brian Blade; bassist John Patitucci; polymath artist Steve Taylor and his wife, painter Deb Taylor; as well as the late Karen Walter Goodwin, who brought *Les Misérables* to Broadway. My complete list of friends and acquaintances who share this multifaceted calling would fill its own book.

We've arrived at the third and last pearl and spark. You can only sustainably fulfill the artist's role across a lifetime with the bundle of ambition, skill, and ability.

When I was a very young Christian and a musician in my midtwenties, the story of Bezalel, found in Exodus 31:2–5, set the course of my artistry to come. Bezalel, the chief artisan, was called by God to create the tabernacle and the ark of the covenant. Here's how it reads: "See, I [the Lord] have chosen Bezalel son of Uri, the son of Hur, of the tribe of Judah, and I have filled him with the Spirit of God, with wisdom, with understanding, with knowledge and with all kinds of skills—to make artistic designs for work in gold, silver and bronze, to cut and set stones, to work in wood, and to engage in all kinds of crafts."

Every artist and human being should pick up on three things immediately: The artisan is filled with the Spirit of God. With this filling of the Spirit come spiritual gifts—wisdom, understanding, knowledge, skill, and ability. And lastly, the work set before the artisan is in service to the Lord (who is always, and in every way, the Master Teacher and Creator).

In Bezalel's case, his story is about a particular kind of work. One related to the Jewish people and their relationship to God with Moses as the prophetic voice. Our stories are contemporary, with the new community of Jesus' followers doing the unique work we are called to and equipped for. But they share a common thread—I think of it as *imagocreatology*. We are made in the image of God to reflect God through what we make, generally and sometimes with particular assignments. And, as part of the artist's life, we're to make an ongoing study of this, gathering ever more trustworthy information to use and pass on.

I am so grateful that Bezalel's story was pointed out at just the right time. If not, my artistic life could have gone in a dramatically different direction.

For example, in 1982, when I was a younger artist and a new follower of Jesus, I quickly picked up on an idea I had repeatedly heard. If I was serious about being a student of Jesus, I had to be all in. Check. But here's how it was being defined. It meant emptying myself of ambition, including being willing to put music down for a time, maybe forever. I kept meeting people who suggested this, had done it, or were presently music-free. The assumption was that you could be too serious about music. So much so that you might have made it an idol. If so, the first commandment demanded that the musician have no other gods before the one true God. Music had to go.

This trend in the wind was human derived and wrong—a misguided, errant idea common to cultural Christianity at the time. Thankfully, I was introduced to a trustworthy and sustainable way of being ambitious.

As it turns out, the artist must have ambition (the arts and the Bible agree). Investing significant time in developing world-class skills is no crime at all. Faithfulness hinges on which definition of *ambition* you're living under and out. Trustworthy ambition is humble, dependent, inclusive of others, and driven by good goals. That little word *good* needs an extensive definition, though. One you'll be learning and piecing together over a lifetime. The clues are already embedded in the Word and Work of Jesus, your calling and artistic tradition, and your dreams for a just and flourishing world. Take the time to continually inventory these clues as you gather them up. Write them down and keep adding them to your collection.

Selfish ambition is what we are to avoid.

With trustworthy definitions in place, I encourage you to make it your ambition to excel at artistic ability out of reverence for God. And for the image of God you bear in the likeness of Jesus, your Teacher. In fact, go ahead and be obsessively ambitious for this excellent end.

Here's another complementary bit to put in the heart and hands.

Never discount the good, personal pleasure of the work. Christians make this error, believing fidelity to God means downplaying the art and the fact that you enjoy making it. Instead, give thanks for it. Art is not simply a utilitarian tool for another goal you find worthier of your time and attention. On the contrary, making art is much more complex, even mysterious, expanding our understanding of goodness, excellence, beauty, and what is real—what contributes to ubiquitous betterment and what works against it.

Respecting your art form, its place in history, and a good vision for its future is essential. It is troubling to me when I hear Christians use the phrase "art for art's sake" disparagingly. I believe that failing to make art for art's sake is failing to be an artist—at least one hoping to fulfill the artist's role in the world.

Would anyone ever say, "Oh, Christian, there you are again practicing the law for the law's sake, baking for the sake of baking, and swimming for the sake of swimming"? Of course not. Remember, "Whatever you do, work at it with all your heart, as working for the Lord. . . . It is the Lord Christ you are serving" (Colossians 3:23–24).

There is no spiritual currency to be gained by devaluing artistic vocations. Artistic apprentices to Jesus are invited to root themselves in the tradition of the chief artist, Bezalel. He was chosen for his honorable work, not because he thought religion was far more important than the arts and telegraphed it at every turn. Quite the opposite. Bezalel was chosen because he was the essential combination of a *skilled artist filled with the Spirit of God*. Don't miss the combination of skill and Spirit. This is the goal of the role.

I encourage you to meditate on service and selflessness as you follow in the footsteps of the Teacher, Jesus. But don't for a minute think this means to downplay your equipping, gifting, skill, and ability—or imagination. Christian artists will sometimes take this posture, feeling it is somehow more spiritual and in keeping with humility. In true goodness, any confidence, gift, or skill you have has been given to you (this is the Giver-and-Gift economy at work).

Suppose you spend any effort posturing modestly and demurely for the camera. In that case, you're missing an opportunity to glorify God—to point to Jesus and say, "You are Love Supreme. Thank you for loving me and letting me in on your artmaking, the remaking of humanity in your image."

The basketball phenom Steph Curry is a public example of what I'm talking about. When he makes a never-done-before shot, Steph knows how improbable the shot would be had God not gifted him for the moment, and had he not done the difficult work of developing skill and ability—teasing out from his gifting every possibility imaginable.

Steph will smile and laugh joyfully as he runs the court, light ablaze. Even he's amazed at making the shots he does. And then what does he do? He taps his heart and points upward, that universal sign among humankind that says, "You did this, God. You put this in me. Thank you. I can't believe I get to do this, to play at this level. May you be glorified in my life and my work." This is public witness through vocation. Art is very much the same.

The arena is not the Chase Center in San Francisco, though, home to Steph's team, the Golden State Warriors. No, the arena is the theater of all God's creativity. It is this grand, cosmic stage in which your gifts expand to meet the world's needs for the world to come.

It all begins with the trailblazer Jesus, our empathetic hero Artist.

He's passing out the details hourly, daily. Stay close to Jesus and what he loves, values, and makes new. This way, you can be briefed as often as needed. Take notes and learn to see every detail of your life in the details Jesus imparts. This is the way you gain wisdom for citizenry and artistry.

Note, here's a critically crucial big idea to keep for life: *learn to extrapolate outward from the missional details of Jesus into every corner of existence.* How does a simple directive like loving your neighbor affect what you choose to learn, how you spend your time and money, whom you admire, what you do with your garbage, and how you make your art? Everything is witness and worship. No corner of your life isn't actively telling a story.

So be aware of the story your artistic life is telling, and give thanks for everything good and trustworthy. Rid yourself of that which isn't. Where's the bar, the standard?

I don't know of a better answer than this one: "Finally, brothers and sisters, whatever is true, whatever is noble, whatever is right, whatever is pure, whatever is lovely, whatever is admirable—if anything is excellent or praiseworthy—think about such things" (Philippians 4:8).

Your role in the world is to observe, pray, and proclaim what is true, noble, right, pure, lovely, admirable, excellent, and praiseworthy, and do so in ways that are uniquely artistic, in keeping with your humanity, gifting, and callings. The good imagination is made for this moment in history. The invitation to participate in the making of all things new is a once-in-a-lifetime offer. Take it and get busy cooperating with the Word and Work of Jesus.

Never tire of doing good. Do not give up. If you continue, in time you will see the fruit of consistent, unrelenting beauty and goodness. And when you see it, you'll know it. It will bring you joy. And without any prompting, you will give thanks and glorify God—a response reflecting the highest form and privilege of artful vocation.

eight

HAVENS OF GRACE

To Those Who Want to Be Hospitable

from Andi

Hospitality, like love, is a word with open-ended meaning. It's a way of life that can't be contained or limited. There's no perfect recipe for its creation. It's not defined by a beautiful photograph in a magazine or a carefully framed social media post. Though the images can be moments within a life of hospitality, they are not the sum of the thing itself. The thing itself is living, growing, responding, changing. It can be intentional and planned, but is also highly improvisational, like jazz.

What is the need of the moment? A cup of cold water? A smile and a greeting? Kindness and respect? Relational connection and help for weary travelers who've been displaced from their home? A Babette's feast of a meal or a peanut butter sandwich?

Is it neighborliness or hospitality or love that I'm talking about?

My thoughts bounce around, traveling through the years, landing here and there. I'm sitting with my neighbor Patsy on her small front porch, catching up. Patsy and her husband, Phillip, lived in a little house between the Harpeth River and our Art House. Phillip was inside, sick and getting sicker. Patsy's heart was breaking every day.

When I walked over that summer evening, I hadn't eaten dinner, though I cooked for guests so often I wore an apron half the time. She asked if I was hungry and disappeared into the house, coming back with a plate, a knife and fork, and a pork chop, left over and still warm from their meal. It was juicy and delicious, fried up in a pan just right.

Patsy was the initiator of our friendship. She introduced herself to me one day when I was out gardening, shortly after they moved into the house. We grew close. We learned about each other's lives and stories. We hugged often and said I love you. When Phillip died, we gathered in their front yard for a simple service, then walked down to the bridge. Patsy threw some of his ashes in the river, the rest of us threw wild Queen Anne's lace gathered from a nearby field.

Less than a year later, Patsy moved out of her house, and we moved out of ours. Eventually we lost touch. Sometimes that's the way of things. I don't like it, but I know it's how life is. It's impossible to stay connected with everyone we've ever been close to. Relational seasons have a lot to do with proximity and timing.

My friend Nancy, who lives three streets and three corner turns away from the house we live in now, was much like Patsy. Friendly. Before we moved in, I had driven over to tend the garden I was about to inherit. Nancy was out walking her dog and stopped at the gate to introduce herself. We've been dear friends now for almost a decade. We walk together on fall and winter afternoons and talk about our daily details the way sisters do.

Our neighbors Asha and Ram are two of the kindest people I've ever met. Asha sometimes packs up containers of home-cooked Indian food and sends them over for our dinner. When two of our grandchildren experienced the 2020 Nashville tornado up close, she blessed them each with a handwritten card and a gift certificate to acknowledge the terrible experience they'd been through. She'd just moved to the neighborhood a few weeks before.

Trisha and Michael live across the street from us. They're generous with care and conversation, and glasses of their best wine. Our next-door neighbors, Kim and Jim, are longtime friends who've come running to us in our most dire emergencies. Even the most casual relationships on my block are meaningful. A hello or a short chat when I walk by is a blessing to me. I come home with my heart a little fuller than when I left, my hunger for connection and belonging a little more satisfied.

Like relationships everywhere, one or two households are more difficult to figure out. Issues are unsolved because conversation is not welcome. Redemption is still off in the distance. I look out my front door at the end of the night and pray for a breakthrough, the restoration of peace. A neighborhood has its quirks like a family and a family is like the world, everyone a neighbor somehow.

In its essence, hospitality is a way of being. You cannot exhaust the possibilities.

For some of you, hospitality is a big part of your vocation. Or you sense that it might be. You are drawn to care for people through place, time, food, and relationship. Beauty matters and you're willing to work for it. These things light up your imagination with possibility and meaning. Your need is to understand the work that's in front of you and enter it with wisdom.

Or perhaps you are someone who wants to live a more welcoming life, but you don't know where to start.

One winter, a graduate student from Vanderbilt University reached out to me after coming to an Art House event. We had a long fireside chat. She wanted a more hospitable life but needed some basic ideas that made sense within the small amount of time she had outside of classes and study.

This woman shared a house with a roommate, but they hardly ever spent time together. I suggested she start there: bake some muffins on a Saturday morning and invite her roommate to breakfast. Simple, but she'd never thought of it before. I sent her home with a photocopy of my favorite apple cinnamon muffins recipe from Marion Cunningham's *The Breakfast Book*, a cookbook I've used so many times the pages are falling out. We talked about inviting one or two people to dinner and trying out an easy recipe. No stress. Just fun. With takeout and delivery now so accessible, I would add that to the mix of possibilities if we were talking today. Whatever is enjoyable, do that. The invitation to relationship is the most important thing. Who is brave enough?

Hospitality is one of the first beautiful things I encountered when I entered the life of the church in the early '80s. It wasn't fancy or formal—just a natural, openhearted, sharing way of life where people took care of each other and welcomed strangers like us. The love they showed our family as they invited us into their homes and shared their lives was like medicine. It was a new kind of community, and it was life-giving.

Hospitality is one of the most beautifully countercultural practices we can live and learn because it's such a powerful communicator of love. In a world that's often exhausting, lonely, and isolating, where we can have a lot of social media "friends" and "followers," we still long for the intimacy of knowing and being known in our real, embodied lives. Hospitality is unexpected and surprising.

And that's why it meant so much to us. We considered ourselves part of the counterculture of the '70s, but the faithful people we met were truly countercultural. They didn't just talk about love in general; they practiced love in specific.

There were names, living rooms, families. We went to a Bible study in Jane Fraga's South Sacramento living room. This kind of gathering was foreign to me, and I was anxious about going. But the group was small and comfortable. Chuck and I sat on the floor with our new Bibles open to the first page of Genesis. The pastor, John Cowan, began at the beginning. After the study we hung out in Jane's kitchen, eating snacks and talking.

I remember calling John before an election and asking him how

I should vote now that I was a Christian. His answer: "Andi, I can't possibly tell you how to vote. You need to study the candidates and the issues and pray. That's the work everyone has to do."

When I needed a babysitter so I could go with Chuck to a gig, the Butera family invited the kids to their house. If someone in the church had a need of some sort, people chipped in with food or with time. We had experienced the help of family and friends before, but this was something else.

We weren't used to a whole community of people behaving that way, and it was instructive, inspiring, and healing. My friend Steve Garber says the best learning is done over the shoulder and through the heart, absorbing a way of life in person. As I joined with them, I learned how to care for people in practical ways during times of grief, illness, and celebration, and before long Chuck and I wanted to open our home too.

It was a tiny beginning to a long vocation in hospitality. I wouldn't have known to use that language then, but in small ways that were organic to our lives, we started responding to a need, and it felt natural. Chuck was beginning to make records and tour in the US and overseas, so when musicians from out of town came to rehearse with him, they slept on our couch and ate breakfast with us.

When the church needed someone else to host a Bible study, we offered our living room. We didn't have much furniture, but we had a lot of green shag carpeting for people to sit on, so we opened our home and never gave a second thought to the fact that everything we had was hand-me-down. We were simply grateful to be together with our children, thankful for the house we rented on Fifty-Seventh Street. We wanted to share it.

As the years went on, and we moved from house to house, we were called to hospitality in ever-deepening ways. People make their way into your heart and you remember them. They become part of your history.

In Sacramento, a young photographer named David Dobson had

been taking pictures of my husband for an album cover. David has been all over the world and done remarkable work. In those days he was young, excited, and tired from traveling. He came over for a tuna fish sandwich and fell asleep on our couch, listening to me read a story to Sam.

Another Dave, this one born in New Zealand and living in London at the time, came to spend a few days with us and experienced his first American Thanksgiving around a squished family table in Yuba City. Sitting across from him, Chuck's aunt Edgule asked David where he was from. To his answer she exclaimed in her thick Okie accent, "Kid, you're way off course!"

Chuck met a lot of people in his travels and often invited them to come round if they came to the West Coast. One Saturday morning in California there was a knock on the door. Paul from New York was standing there. "Charlie gave me your address and told me to stop by if I was ever in the area. Here I am!" It was Paul's lucky day. I just happened to be making pancakes.

And then came Nashville and the Art House. My journals are full of serendipitous stories.

We'd have houseguests and a recording session in the studio. I'd make food. Right around mealtime, one or two other people might drop by out of the blue, and we'd all sit together around the table. I can't think of an instance like that when the conversation wasn't interesting or the laughter not plentiful. And the food? There is truly a loaves-and-fishes phenomena in those moments of surprise.

I remember Micah coming to the kitchen door on two different occasions when I was baking cookies for an event: chocolate chip, oatmeal, snickerdoodles, coffee chocolate brownies. Lots and lots of baking. Micah was a young singer-songwriter, newly married, delivering flowers for a florist to help pay the bills. He had a delivery in our area. Each time, it was a happy coincidence that I had baked goods coming out of the ovens and cooling on the counters. I'd take a break, we'd sit at the kitchen table with our cookies, and we'd talk about many things. I wondered at the time, *Is the smell of baking cookies floating around the air in Bellevue?* What is it that draws a person to come at just the right moment?

Other days I wondered what it is that draws someone to show up at a very inconvenient time, when you can't possibly tend to them because you're already overloaded or anxious about a deadline. But when hospitality is vocation, you learn that sometimes the interruptions are part of the work. You move with the Spirit.

As I grew in years and understanding, I knew from my own life how frustrating it was to be in real need and have no one to talk to. Without an appointment, you can't get to a pastor, a therapist, or even a friend. So I would pray under my breath, "Lord, will there be enough if I stop and attend? Please help me trust you to provide."

In responding to my callings as they developed, I learned to welcome people in all of these ways—to cook for them, prepare guest rooms, sit in long conversations, turn from other work to receive an unexpected person, and help host the occasional larger gathering featuring theologians, writers, teachers, actors, and musicians. Our work was artist-centric, but most of the gatherings were for anyone who wanted to explore what an artful, faithful life might mean for them.

When our children grew up and left home, we had more rooms available, and hospitality became even more intense. In the doing of all this hospitality, I could see how much it mattered in people's lives—from sitting with someone over a cup of coffee to more involved encounters. Simplicity and complexity—there was a time for each.

I also learned that hospitality was my strength and it was my weakness. It was a life rich in relationships and experiences that couldn't be repeated in any other setting. I loved when someone came as a stranger and left as a friend. I loved imagining menus and creating in the kitchen. I loved sitting up late with houseguests talking and laughing around the table. And I loved the privilege of holding others' stories in prayerful, sacred space. It was all a privilege, full of meaning and purpose.

At the same time, taking care of people all the time was hard, demanding, and exhausting. Sometimes I did it really well, and sometimes I just wanted everyone to go away and leave me alone. Along with the beautiful, rewarding side of hospitality, there's a broader reality: loss of privacy, immature or thoughtless houseguests, and people who don't think to give space to their hosts—if you're an introvert, that one hits hard.

Sheets and towels get ruined from makeup and hair products. Some houseguests eat your food night after night and leave you with the dirty dishes every time. And hospitality happens in the midst of a life lived—in the midst of family emergencies, the demands of other work, fights with your spouse, and hard patches with your kids. These are real things. They're not easy things. And over time, frustration and resentment can build.

We often had people in our home for weeks at a time without a break. When that happened and my negative thoughts and attitudes confronted me, I had to go back to the gospel again and again. I needed a right theology deeply planted in my mind and heart, reminding me that my standing is in grace and my acceptance comes through Christ alone, not through my performance.

If you practice hospitality enough, it will begin to look like everyday life, not perfection. True, biblical hospitality is born of grace—grace for the giver and grace for the receiver. The words of Jesus in Matthew 25 always bring me back to the essentials: "For I was hungry and you gave me something to eat, I was thirsty and you gave me something to drink, I was a stranger and you invited me in. . . . Whatever you did for one of the least of these brothers and sisters of mine, you did for me" (vv. 35, 40).

Dear reader, as you think on these things, know that you will never run out of opportunities to meet those basic needs in your own households and neighborhoods, on the streets of your city, and across the world. These scriptures have a wide application. The message is clear that even the smallest act of caring for another human being in a life-giving way is an enormous expression of love to God himself. It's about meeting human need where we find it, and we find it in the life God gives us.

There are times to invite people to our table, offering the gift of beauty, good food, and rich fellowship. Robert Farrar Capon, author of the unique and wonderful book *The Supper of the Lamb*, wrote that we can allow a shared meal and a tasty glass of wine "its sovereign power to turn evenings into occasions, to lift eating beyond nourishment to conviviality, and to bring the race, for a few hours at least, to that happy state where men are wise and women beautiful, and even one's children begin to look promising." Thus, Capon continued, we might join with God and "delight . . . in the resident goodness of creation."[1] Take or leave the wine, the gathering is a powerful good.

There are other times when people come and we have dirty dishes overflowing the sink, unmade beds, toys all over the floor, and stacks of mail on the counters. That's a gift, too, because it's real life, and it means we can all relax and be human together.

But whether it's a beautiful celebration or a more ordinary day of inviting another person into our full and messy lives for a chat, hospitality is work. It's work to prepare the way and clean up after, and work to consciously turn away from other things to be truly present in the room, in the conversation.

We are more aware than ever of the ministry of presence. It's a precious gift in our distracted world and increasingly hard to give for the very same reason. But if you're on the receiving end, if it is your time of need, there is almost no better gift than being listened to, feeling heard, and not being alone.

In general, in both church culture and the larger society, there is one big issue that gets in the way of a full comprehension of caregiving work and vocation. Work continues to be largely understood only in terms of a work/compensation model. And most of the caregiving that takes place in everyday life is not paid labor. The mother or father caring for children and family life, the person who's always meeting the practical needs of neighbors and friends, the work of hospitality . . . there are a million different versions of what caregiving can look like. It's hard work and it's creative work, but so much of it takes place quietly, without much fanfare. The results are seen, felt, and enjoyed by others, but it's rare for folks to really notice or think about the labor that went on behind the scenes.

Biblically speaking, work has an intrinsic value of its own when it's carried out to satisfy genuine need. The value of someone's work has nothing to do with whether or not it has a paycheck attached to it. It's crucial for caregivers to understand this, to learn a holistic theology of work, to know their labor matters to God and to the flourishing of families and societies. Everyone needs to know their work matters. It's wearying to feel invisible to the world or to the people in your own household. But if you can latch on to the truth that caring for human life is a very powerful work that actually changes the shape of people's lives and the way they experience the world, you will have a vision that can hold you even in the midst of dismissive cultural attitudes.

When our imaginations are captured by the idea of creating good stories in the lives of the people we've been given to love, a world of possibility opens up. It must be said that a lot of caregiving work is tedious and repetitive. Washing endless loads of laundry, a thousand trips to the grocery store, cleaning up after children, all the bits and pieces required to care for a spouse or friend who's battling illness. But if we can keep in mind the bigger story we're creating, it goes a long way in bringing meaning to the details.

All of this takes time and energy; it takes the hours and years of our lives. When hospitality is an ever-present reality, there's a sobering need to think of how we might respond without losing ourselves in the process.

In 2015, after twenty-four years of Art House life, my husband and I moved out of our beloved home and handed the work over to Nate and Cassie Tasker, a younger couple whom we love and trust. During the writing of this book, the Taskers have moved, too, and the property has been sold. It's no longer an Art House but is being used for other good purposes. We're all grateful for that. But in the years that we were transitioning out and the Taskers were moving in, we talked frequently about how to have a life that's filled with hospitality and its work, while living wisely in the midst of it. This is what I recommend to anyone with a similar vocation:

1. As you practice hospitality or caregiving of any kind, also practice self-care.

   I wonder if this term has become so common that it's lost its good meaning or become watered down with overuse? Here is what I'm aiming for: don't let your own needs get lost. Being drained and depleted is not a good gift for anyone. If you're called to a life of nurturing others, you need nurture too. Be intentional about replenishing and filling your tank.

   I've always looked for the small things that bring pleasure and care because those are doable in daily life. Accessibility is important. The big things like vacations are great, but they come only once a year, if they come at all.

   For each of us, our list of the small things will be different. For me, it means respecting my need to read, write in my journal, spend time with peer friends, and take walks or swim laps. A bubble bath with a novel goes a long way. I listen to interesting podcasts when I'm cooking or cleaning up. Having my mind engaged changes the way it feels to do the dishes or fold laundry. And a classic self-care practice like getting a massage is no longer a luxury for me but a necessity, part of taking care of a creaky, aging body.

   I was helped along the way by the wisdom in Eugene Peterson's book *The Contemplative Pastor*. He wrote, "I venture to prescribe appointments for myself to take care of the needs not only of my body but also of my mind and emotions, my spirit and imagination. One week, in addition to daily half-hour conferences with Saint Paul, my calendar reserved a two-hour block of time with Fyodor Dostoevsky. My spirit needed that as much as my body ten years ago needed the physical therapist. If nobody is going to prescribe it for me, I will prescribe it for myself."[2]

Sometimes a small tweak toward nurture can make a hospitality commitment better. One of the lovely things I've done in my work over the years is meet with younger people in mentoring friendships.

From the moment we moved into the Art House, I received phone calls, letters, and in-person inquiries: *Will you mentor me? Can we get together for coffee?* It happened so often, for so many years, that I came to understand that spending time in this way, mostly with women, on a walk, in a coffee shop, or at my house, was a big part of the life I was being given. I valued it and made room for it.

I never had any idea what mentoring meant in a formal sense. I met with people and talked about life, and then did it again and again. I kept them in my prayers. Some of the relationships were only for a season, but others became lifetime friendships. We've grown up together; we've gone through hard things. The care has been mutual.

2. Think about creating a sustainable vocation with boundaries in mind.

There are so many times when you can't control the circumstances. You can't control how other people in your family schedule their lives and how that affects you. You can't control family or friend emergencies. And you don't really know what shape you'll be in when the time comes to welcome someone.

One weekend I was getting ready to host a small group of women whom I didn't know. I shared a mutual friend with one of them and we'd met briefly, but the rest were total strangers. Together, they had read my book *Real Love for Real Life* and reached out to see if we could talk. It sounded like fun, but since they lived four hours away and one of them had a new baby, I invited them to spend the night.

As I prepared food and beds in anticipation of their arrival, I felt drained from an already long week, but they were on their way and there was no turning back.

Out of a very honest place, I prayed: "Lord, I can't welcome them in my own strength. I don't have any. Please give me your strength and help me welcome them as Christ. Bless the relationships about to be born."

That weekend turned out to be an important beginning to my long relationship with them. God blessed our time, we became friends, and the women came back in different configurations for the next several years before they all scattered to different areas of the country. To this day they are all very dear to me. That weekend I learned one more lesson about the mutual gift of hospitality—entering in as strangers and parting as friends. You never know the good surprises that might be waiting when you open the door, even when you're not the best version of yourself starting out!

The unknowns of hospitality notwithstanding, when you can schedule things carefully in advance, do it inside boundaries that keep your health, marriage, family life, and friendships intact. And hold space for the other aspects of who you are. Don't lose yourself.

I so often pushed my calling as a writer to the side because the needs of hospitality were more immediate—people's need for food and shelter spoke louder than the unfinished page. I did get writing done, but there were many long pauses in the work. Even months-at-a-time pauses.

I always held those two things in tension: the calling to hospitality, which is so much about immersing with people, and the calling to write, which needs the opposite—time alone to work and focus. I never did strike a perfect balance, and I don't know that I could have. But if I had to do it over again, I would set more boundaries on the front end. Intentionally protecting the other parts of who we are is crucial.

3. Practice hospitality with a Sabbath mindset.

One of my husband's former students at Lipscomb University once told me she'd been practicing the Sabbath and it changed the way she was experiencing university life. She didn't feel overwhelmed in the way that she had before. I love the way she described it: "Sabbath is counterintuitive. It's a trust fall." Taking one day out of seven to cease our worry and our work is indeed a trust fall, but it's essential.

Every worker needs rest and play. We need to let down our hair, take a nap, do something fun, read quietly. As hospitality providers, we're often welcoming strangers, but we also need to be with people we already know—with our friends and our families. We need time alone with God and with ourselves.

People who do caregiving work of any kind tend to keep doing it all the time, and people let them do it all the time. This is not an easy one to figure out in situations where the needs just don't stop—when there are children or elderly parents to care for, when a spouse travels a lot and you're left alone to care for everyone.

But it is worthwhile to try, to pray for creative solutions and ask for help. If we don't pay attention to the needs of our bodies, minds, and spirits over a long period of time, we will become mentally and physically exhausted. It's just a fact.

4. Take sabbaticals.

If I were at the beginning of a hospitality ministry centered in my home, I would scatter a few sabbaticals into the rhythm of the years. With time, experience, and a seminary degree, I understood that my work was holistic, immersive pastoral care. The standard for pastor sabbaticals is two or three months at least every seven years for rest and renewal. We tried a partial sabbatical once but continued all our other work, so in the end, it wasn't very helpful. A true sabbatical would have been life-giving.

In summary, practicing self-care, establishing boundaries, asking for God's strength in our weakness, and practicing Sabbath and sabbatical are anchors. They are practices to begin with and truths to return to when things get out of whack and we need realignment, wisdom for the road ahead.

Finally, it's good to know that hospitality changes with the seasons of life. You can't always do things in the same way. And that's freeing, something I'm learning to embrace.

A month after handing over the operation of Art House to Nate and Cassie and moving to a new neighborhood, I was still unpacking boxes, but we were functional. I had the urge to invite two of my longtime women friends, Kim and Michelle, for dinner. It was late summer so I bought fresh vegetables from a farm stand down the street and a tiny lemon cake from Whole Foods. I roasted salmon and okra in separate pans, layered fresh mozzarella and ribbons of basil on a platter of sliced heirloom tomatoes, and steamed some crookneck and zucchini squash.

We ate on the porch of my little courtyard garden, sipping our drinks and talking until late at night. In our previous setting, I'd longed for time around the table with old and dear friends, but it was hard to find, particularly in our final decade at the Art House. After cooking for recording sessions and houseguests, I rarely had the energy left over to invite anyone else. Making dinner for my friends that night was a gift for me, the blessing of their company a sign of good things to come.

As we settled into our lives in a more urban setting, the change in location opened the way to a simpler kind of community, one that was easily within our reach. I still cooked, but we also met friends in restaurants or shared take-out meals. Having options helped us be with people, old friends and new. It's a hospitality of time shared without a lot of fuss.

We got used to enjoying the comfort of easy, back-and-forth hospitality with our next-door neighbors. Once a week or so, one of us would send a text, "Can we get together for a sip?" We'd go to their house, or they'd come to ours, and we'd sit with something to drink and catch up, most likely with our slippers and comfy clothes on. We might share crackers and cheese or popcorn for dinner. It was always casual and usually spur-of-the-moment. While life in our other house was weighted with people coming to us, this mutual hospitality was lovely for us all.

And then, of course, the COVID-19 pandemic came and our ways of being with people changed for a time. I learned how sweet it is to drag a chair to the sidewalk and get to know a neighbor I hadn't spent much time with before. With family and friends, when we couldn't gather in all our usual ways, we got creative and moved our celebrations outdoors, even when it was cold and everyone had to bundle up. All that mattered was being with those we love. Gratitude replaced complaint. And for all of us in the human family, we're learning long lessons about the loving ways of intellectual hospitality, as we open our minds and hearts to curiosity, ask questions, and listen with respect.

With hospitality as with life, seasons change and we adjust. The topic expands and we grow. Hospitality is big enough to extend across a lifetime, and small enough to elevate a simple cup of tea and conversation into something important. The needs we come across, including our own, will guide us. Whether sharing a meal or an afternoon or providing a bed for the night, there's a time for everything. A time to offer and a time to rest, a time for family and a time for strangers, a time to refresh others and a time to be refreshed.

nine

TALKING ABOUT JESUS IN THE PUBLIC SQUARE

To the Writer and Public Speaker of Any Kind

from Charlie

By the year 2014, it felt as if I'd spent a decade or more mostly keeping quiet about what people call *spiritual things*. And by *spiritual things*, they usually mean metaphysics, ontology, cosmology, epistemology, and theology—whether they name and define these ten-dollar words or not. For me, my whole concept of spiritual things is rooted in that storied, ubiquitous, historical person, Jesus. I believe he is who he says he is. If you understand what I mean by this, then you know it's an extraordinary thing to say and believe about reality. One that comes with the ordinary and respected tension of living in a pluralistic country, as well as the unwanted stress of living in a culture-war zone.

The latter is an ever-consequential, daily, soul-sucking problem. Especially so when soldiers of the war think Jesus is their five-star General. The co-opting of the Jesus name for something other than love of God and neighbor has a long and bloody past. But this is what 2 Corinthians 11:4 calls "another Jesus" (MSG).

There's a deeper, longer story of the authentic Jesus who prioritized love of God and neighbor that exists without the media, though. This is the Jesus and the story I belong to.

Belief and trust in this Jesus has birthed my life and all its attending stories for more than four decades. I had, for a ten-year period, deliberately chosen to keep some of these stories quieter and private. Other than a few interviews and the occasional post at the *Art House America* blog, I'd required of myself what I'd so often hoped for from others—a little reserve, maybe even silence. And so, on the topics of God, people, and place, interdependent topics of reality I'm very passionate about, I had gone mostly quiet.

For a time, quiet was my protest. I think I was fatigued and embarrassed by my impression that the majority of people who write or speak in public, using language and terminology associated with Jesus and Christianity, are not the spokespeople the world would benefit from hearing. I'm not putting forth the idea that I am. I thought it was intolerably noisy then, and my reaction was retreat. Little did I know that the future was about to roar in ways I had yet to experience. Silence would no longer be an option.

During my ten-year quiet, Andi and I would often say to each other, "I can think of many people I know and love that I wish friends and neighbors could hear from concerning Jesus." The trajectory of our lives has brought us in contact with people of remarkable artistic, philosophical, and theological vision. We want everyone to know them! But few of them are mainstreamed. And most who are vocal, using explicit language in winsome, thoughtful ways, are often speaking and writing only to those who are already committed to the conversation—an unfortunate effect of genre and branding, social media algorithms, confirmation bias, and information overload in need of trustworthy librarians and curators.

Which is why viewing the internet and the social media giants as the public square is a truly naïve utopian notion. The web is less the egalitarian information superhighway promised in the '90s and more the streets of New York City—where you could live your whole life in an apartment in the Upper East Side and miss that the best information about the most important things is found at the corner of Bank Street and Waverly Place in the Village—perhaps that's overstating the importance of a good dinner. The point is, to maximize NYC, you need a friend, a curator, a recommendation, a tip. Getting at the Jesus story of God, people, and cosmos in a coherent, believable way also requires trusted community, expert curators, and Jesus followers who accurately handle the Word and Work of God—the unique revelation of the Jesus story and the general revelation of God's creativity. While the responsibility falls to every follower of Jesus, those called to write and speak in public vocationally experience unique and confounding challenges.

As a follower of Jesus, writing or speaking in public requires expressing your understanding of God, people, and cosmos, doesn't it? Whether explicit or implicit. In a culture-war zone, a single word or sentence can be, will be, interpreted as a shot fired. God-talk assures there will be return fire. If the Jesus name is in the mix, expect drones and missiles. For good reason though. There's that pesky *other Jesus* out there making headlines. Remember, the name *Jesus* was all over the January 6 US Capitol insurrection. While windows broke and alarms rang, one woman convicted of illegally demonstrating inside the Capitol and jailed for sixty days was filmed saying, "Here we are, in the name of Jesus!" After taking over the Senate chambers, one of the insurrectionists standing on the Senate dais shouted, "Jesus Christ, we invoke your name!"[1]

While it's heartbreaking how divisive people can be when it comes to their opinions about Jesus or the idea of God in general, empathy should be at the ready. It is possible to hold a strong position and empathy for your detractors, and to clearly understand why they think you're an untrustworthy actor. And you can do all of this and still believe there's nothing so destructive as when conversation is reduced to *You're an idiot if you believe this. You're an idiot if you don't.*

I have the benefit of being part of an artistic spiritual tradition. History is filled with Jesus-following artists and classic autodidact spiritual seekers. Similar to the late John Coltrane and Johnny Cash, and contemporaries Bono and Dylan, the great American songwriter Paul Simon keeps bringing his spiritual search into earshot of the public, mostly via his lyrics.

A few years ago, Paul Simon met with one of the people I do trust to speak out loud, the well-known British theologian John Stott (now passed away). I was in the greenroom backstage at a U2 concert. I stood around a table with friends Steve Garber and the late U2 chaplain Jack Heaslip. We listened as journalist David Brooks told a story. The writer had published a very favorable op-ed piece in the *New York Times* about Stott. Not a common occurrence at all. It wasn't long before David heard from a native New Yorker, perhaps one of NYC's and the world's most famous musicians, Paul Simon. The story goes that the musician wanted to know if David was for real. Did he really think that any Christian could be taken seriously? Wasn't the very idea of allowing for such a thing antithetical to reason, to pluralism, to the progress of society? And so on.

David set up a meeting between the Englishman and the New Yorker. They met and the New Yorker was given time to vent about why Christians can't be taken seriously. For example: their unholy alliances, incessant meddling, exclusive truth claims, far-right politics, homophobia, lack of sophistication, warmongering, and just plain stupidity. After a while the Brit acknowledged the occurrence of all of it common to the human condition and said something to the effect of "What about Jesus? Let's turn our attention to him."

Jesus asked his disciples, "Who do people say I am?" This is the kind of question that reproduces questions. People say many things about who Jesus is. But who do *I* say he is? What did Jesus say about himself? What can be known about his mission? What are his followers supposed to concern themselves with? Am I living congruent with this mission on earth? And so the questions go. I would say no Christian should be found writing and speaking in public without unclichéd answers to these questions in their marrow. That's my dream, anyway. One dramatically unrealized.

There is the other Jesus and then there is the mess of those of us who are following and failing.

It is easy to become distracted by all the incongruent and contradictory stories people who claim association with Jesus are telling through their confused and broken lives (mine included). Awareness of the wreckage is important. You want to take care in choosing the people you team up with and give your allegiance to—and, as writers and speakers, endorse. But don't stare too long at the mess. Look to Jesus and carry on. Whenever the wreckage distracts me, I've learned to turn my attention to two sobering questions: What kind of story am I telling through the life I've been given? And have I faithfully front-loaded humility and generative love into all my being and doing?

And so, with more than a little caution, beginning in 2014, I took another shot at being a public person who holds to ideas about the existence of God; the mission, glory, and shame of humanity; and the earth as a remarkable place of redemption and possibility. I put a name to this experiment: *The Hope of Humble Explicitness.*

Off I went, writing in public, having a public voice again. Very quickly, I came face-to-face with unique challenges and lessons I was about to learn or relearn. To keep track of my experiment, I wrote a brief summary of my thoughts after a few weeks of reentering the public conversation as a person and writer:

1. Writing in public is hard work! It takes time (and for me, prayer) to choose words with care—to give thought and empathy to a variety of potential readers. I want to get better at it.
2. It's a huge challenge to critique, compare, and contrast in public and not marginalize or disenfranchise anyone. Negating/

dismissing a person, institution, worldview, etc. in order to put our own thoughts/agenda on offer comes too easy to the human family. Unfortunately, it's difficult for us to see clearly when we're in the middle of doing it—especially when putting someone in their place with your blinding intelligence feels like such a winning tool for argument. The pure folly of it.

3. Wrestling with how to create loving and issue-explicit public speech/text in the post-internet/information age is a challenge worth facing. Knowing and being known, hearing and being heard is neighbor love in action. And for our time in history, it's bringing the already expansive neighborhood near—literally taking all people in all places seriously.

4. Writing in public (including commenting on what others have written) involves a varied and mixed bag of the related "-ologies," such as theology, philosophy, sociology, psychology, epistemology, ontology, as well as politics, gender and sexuality, and, of course, communication and conflict resolution, manners and civility, hermeneutics, postmodernism and literary deconstructionism (should I keep going?). Even in a passionate blog entry or comment, it helps to be aware of the place of all of this in setting the stage for a winsome public conversation, and writing with magnanimity so that anyone, anywhere might read and engage. Turning back to number 1—this is hard work, but worth it.

5. To live on the planet in our time is to live in a neighborhood composed of the most exaggerated hyphenate pluralism and syncretism the world has ever known. Because of this, to get particular about our love and language may mean reimagining what it means to speak and write with integrity—old words and phrases may need to be replaced and thought through afresh. While in the midst of learning new ways, there is potential for confusion and anger. For example, taking great care with language for one person becomes evasion of confession

for another. Refusing to clearly nail down what team you're playing for can really anger and exasperate some people. As a musician, I've experienced this most of my adult life. Contrary to how we sometimes bear witness, living with each other gracefully is not a competitive contact sport.

6. Sometimes words are simply worn out from overuse and collect associations that shut down communication. And even more complicated is that the words are no longer buttressed solely by etymology (though personally I wish we'd all revisit this); they are now, oftentimes, more about perceived (though etymologically inaccurate) meaning and emotion. Such as how people feel about the words they hear and read, not what the words actually mean etymologically, currently.

And so it began.

———

In October 2014 I led a conversation at Hutchmoot in Nashville, a weekend event sponsored by the Rabbit Room, filled with discussion centered on art, the way of Christian curiosity and discipleship, and the work and pleasure of telling stories across a range of subjects and mediums.

My topic was "The Whole World Is Listening In"—just another entry point to the new mission I'd begun earlier in the year. Because of our unique time in history, if we are speaking and/or writing, putting our art and heart out into the data stream, the whole world is listening in—at least potentially. There are no private moments and no back rooms. The planet and every means by which information travels is the new and very noisy public square. This really is the most pluralist and syncretized global culture the world has ever known. So, if the whole world is listening in, how should we adapt our communication, if at all? This is a question directed at all citizens, not only writers and public speakers.

The Hutchmoot keynote speaker was poet and author Luci Shaw. Luci is a charter member of the Chrysostom Society of writers and the author of many volumes of poetry and nonfiction, including *Breath for the Bones* and *Adventure of Ascent*. Andi and I love Luci's heart, intellect, and moxie—and the Shaw imprint she and her late husband, Harold, founded is where we were first published. She's an inspiration to all who meet her. As is her husband, John Hoyte, most infamous for walking an elephant over the French Alps from Montmélian, France, to Susa, Italy, testing a possible path used by Hannibal to attack Rome with his army and a herd of elephants. These two are not your average octogenarians.

We had a lively and profitable conversation surrounding "The Whole World Is Listening In" topic. Winding down to a close, two longtime friends and fellow seminarians each asked a provocative question. One wanted to know if I had any forecasts for new technology/ software on the horizon that may help or worsen our ability to communicate in the future. The other was curious to know if I thought large-format communication like books would vanish altogether—a topic of value to Hutchmoot, a community committed to publishing books—including *Real Love for Real Life*, written by Andi, and Art House founding member Douglas McKelvey's *Every Moment Holy*.

So it was that the Q&A closed with prognostications.

With respect to books and reading, I'm in a very small minority (as is Hutchmoot). A 2014 Pew Research study had only 28 percent of Americans reading eleven or more books in a year, and a quarter of the population don't read *any* books[2] (I checked pewresearch.org again in 2023, and the percentages remain roughly the same).

On the opposite side of trending, I read at least fifty books a year, for enjoyment and work (as I'm always involved in some sort of research). Still, even though I'm pro-book, I'm more concerned with the future of what I might call a pro-people and pro-planet literacy. I do not read to be bookish but rather to know people and the world better. Books are just one means of accessing the thoughts, opinions, imagination, and research of others. And though I love the physical libraries in our home, I'm not particular about how or where I read. I use the various digital libraries available online, read books on my iPad, and listen to books via Audible.

I want to be an imaginative, well-informed contributor to the ubiquitous betterment of all people and this spinning ball of land and ocean we occupy. I'm interested in whatever aids me and others in this pursuit. Even though I read books daily, I read text on the internet as much or more. The internet, search engines, and large language models such as ChatGPT are aggregating the largest book the world has ever known. Or the largest library, however you wish to look at it. Anyone with the weakest internet connection can access the strongest of ideas (and lies).

This being so, my first prognostication was that all software and hardware (including wearables) will continue the trend of access to seemingly unlimited data and knowledge, as well as the collective imagination and creativity of humanity in general. The ideology of all communication software and technology will continue to be based in boundaryless access and choice. Anyone with a connection to the grid can access a neighbor's thoughts on Common Core standards of education, the trip a friend took to Vietnam, the food and drink a cousin enjoyed at a farm-to-table restaurant, and the actual specifics of critical race theory. All of this, I offered, will continue in new ways and forms yet to arrive—and yes, boomers might even do well to imagine Facebook fading into the digital sunset. It really could happen. "Why do you think they try to snatch up their younger competitors?" I asked, thinking of Snapchat.

Ironically, this boomer took a swipe at Facebook not knowing that in the not-too-distant future I would spend some time working for Meta (Facebook and Instagram), helping to create their Meta Music Initiative platform. Thankfully, they didn't go belly-up.

What's really interesting, though, I told the audience then, is that our radically complex, information-drenched world will continue to demonstrate an increasing intolerance of complexity and lengthy communication (such as a book). Therein is the rub and irony. All of this available information, never seen before in recorded history, has decreased our patience and attention spans. "Keep it simple, stupid" (KISS) is the tacit mantra of the most complex culture ever known. Championing concise communication aside, isn't this part of the explanation for the nine- and, wait for it, eighteen-minute TED-talkish norm for public speaking that has overtaken our conferences and retreats?

I assured the Hutchmoot crowd that books would continue to be created, yet most likely read by fewer and fewer people. All the while, more citizens will have access to the big book of the internet through an inexhaustible invention of not only software, hardware, and wearables but the refining of universal accessibility for all—and the global citizens will make their voices heard and their images seen. Which is, in part, the making of world culture, no matter how niche the contribution may seem.

We now know ourselves and each other in edited snapshots, sound bites, and carefully framed photo ideals. We are curating the versions of ourselves we want others to experience. Our desire to be present with people is waning. As it does, we miss out on the complexity of humanity, in the subtle nuances of our glory *and* our shame. Instead of engaging with love, this micro-capture epistemology of posting and commenting has become our preferred way of knowing.

With this in mind, I shared my conviction that this never-seen-before democratizing of expertise, information, and unlimited access will not make us better human beings. Instead, I was more convinced that the consequences of information overload and microepistemology will be more class and caste distinction—a new way of doing the haves and have-nots, rather than truly democratized, neighbor-love equality, justice, and equity. Progress is never our healer. Information is not the same as neighborly, loving communication.

Whatever the future holds for how we communicate and learn,

none of it will matter if we have not loved well, if our words and images fail to generate goodness, no matter how proximate our earnest effort.

> Then I remember—love, not cramped in where it goes,
> May be reversed, enlarged by love's complicity,
> Its give and take. The sumptuous fragrance of a rose
> Accepts no close confinement or captivity.
> The tide that outward ebbs, turns then and inward flows,
> And what I offer you, you'll multiply to me.[3]

What have I learned in a decade since returning to writing and speaking in public? Has my hope of humble explicitness been realized or dashed? Has what I've offered to the world in love and empathy been multiplied to me in kind?

If you are a writer or public speaker of any variety, then you already have some idea as to how I'll answer the last question, don't you?

Let's address the proverbial pachyderm first. If we thought 2014 was a minefield for the expression of ideas, and specifically Jesus-centric ones, the worst was coming, and then coming some more.

Remember these words and phrases? *Seriously, not literally.* Coined by Salena Zito in the *Atlantic* in 2016—meaning, to take the words of someone seriously enough to affect reality, but not to accept those same words as literal or real (i.e., their most basic sense and meaning).[4] Which leads nicely to *alternative facts*, coined by Kellyanne Conway in 2017.

In this environment, words, and, more to the point, what is real, came under constant attack: *hoax, witch hunt, unprecedented, misinformation, fake news* are just a few words and phrases we heard daily. Let's not forget *dog whistles, gaslighting,* and *clickbait.* Or *confirmation bias* and *false equivalence.* Fans of Aristotle must've been elated to see Greek thought make such a startling reappearance in daily life. I was reacquainted with the fallacies (not all that Aristotle cataloged, but the hits).

You'll recognize these: *Red herring*—misdirection, changing the subject, distracting from an issue by pointing to another—this is the *whataboutism* we keep hearing about. *Strawman*—intentionally misrepresenting someone or their ideas so you can easily knock them down. *Slippery slope*—absurd extrapolation; arguing without any merit that a small choice will lead to massive (and perhaps terrible) consequences. *Begging the question*—circular reasoning, where one begins with what they are trying to prove. Here the premise needs evidence as much as the conclusion, but the user has none, a.k.a., *chicken and egg*. Lastly, *post hoc*—false causation or *one thing leads to another*—confusing correlation with causation. Musicians who like wintergreen mints are more likely to succeed than those who don't. Therefore, if we convince all musicians to eat wintergreen mints, more musicians will be successful. False.

This exercise could go on for pages. Point made, though, correct? If you're in the words business, or simply interested in how society interacts and uses words, the past decade has been prodigiously incidental and just plain . . . strange. Some have referred to it as a "knowledge crisis." So not just a problem of how we use and perceive words, but how we know what we know, wholesale. I will add that, in my lifetime, this is the most topsy-turvy language and epistemology season since the 1960s into the early 1970s.

For citizens of the world, and specifically followers of Jesus, who maintain that words have meaning, and ideas, consequences, I've identified what I think is a positive outcome in this "unprecedented" stirring of the wordy waters.

There is a renewed interest in, and respect for, truth and facts. After a century and more of attacks on the idea of objective truth, or trustworthy facts on any given subject, these human helpers have made a comeback. Not in their older enlightenment form, or a hammering of the absolute so much as in a new, more carefully defined, humble, and generative form.

A large portion of American citizens seem to be collectively discovering that we need the simple distinction between truth and lies, and the option to assert that, with any given subject, all personal truths (or understanding, if you will) are not equal, and by definition someone's alternate facts must cease to be named as facts. If not immediately, then in the near future.

A truth/untruth, fact/nonfact contrast is sustained by allowing for an environment of freedom. The freedom to think, speak, and act in noble and ignoble ways. Laws are the guardrails. Though lacking much in description, in general, this is the American experiment, isn't it? Whether in America, or globally, the respect for and encouragement of freedom for all human flourishing (or floundering) is wholly dependent on us though, isn't it? In a sense, some part of global health is dependent on my spiritual, mental, and physical health. My "knowledge crisis" is a tiny slice of the world's.

Knowing I cannot control the commitments and responses of the other eight billion residents of earth, I've asked myself: What do I control? What is the condition of my spiritual, mental, physical health? If I'm experiencing a knowledge crisis of some sort, what exactly is it? And lastly, what is this "more carefully defined, humble, and generative form" of reasoned and faithful truth I alluded to a few sentences back? Why and how am I committed to it?

Before I reveal how I answer these questions generally, let me remind myself and you, dear readers, that we are doing this deep dive in order to be better, more humble storytellers, as writers and speakers. This is the mission.

What do I control? I control my own individual thoughts, behavior, and maturity. I am, as I hope my neighbors will be, a responsible adult with agency. This leans into the very old bits of biblical advice about getting and keeping my own house in order (at death's door or otherwise) and removing logs from my eyes. There's also the issue of effectual spiritual maturity manifesting itself in all sorts of good fruit, including self-control.

So there's the personal. But there's also the possessional—that is, all I've been given control over to love and care for, that whole stewardship thing that cultural apologists like me keep bringing up. This is what I can wrap my arms around. But there's one more thing I can control that I can barely wrap my mind around. On its own it doesn't look like it amounts to much, because it is so seldom quantifiable for the average person. But here it is: I control the world. We control the world. You, me, we just have one eight-billionth of a say. How? Through our word and work, what we speak with the tongue, write, and create with the whole of our lives. We Christians have to be very careful how we think about and effectuate this control, though. One false assumption and move, and we can easily be in the company of conquerors, theocrats, bullies, and self-dealing politicians. All control must pass through the portal of love as defined by Jesus and his summary of the law of love.

What does this ask of us, as writers and anyone who makes their voice heard in public? Above all, humility. Self-control, by definition, requires self-knowledge. For me, this means a general understanding of my strengths and weaknesses, implicit and explicit assumptions and social drivers, mental and physical health, affirmed gifts and talents, and a forgiven inventory of the extraordinary amount of mistakes I've made. As I've written elsewhere, quoting songwriter Kris Kristofferson, I am a "walking contradiction, partly truth and partly fiction."[5]

Humility takes up residence in us most often through humbling circumstances balancing our natural tendencies toward pride and arrogance (even if the latter are empty swagger and bluster). It also creates a mind-heart ecosystem that makes saying *Sorry* and *I was wrong* just a little bit easier.

Here's an admission of bias: I'm not attracted to writers and speakers who fail to winsomely demonstrate the ability to mix confidence in their abilities and content with caution and concern for their own contradictions, or potential to serve up inerrant certainties (that are neither). I don't trust them. Why? It's not human. And from this Christian's understanding, it's not congruent with reality for a follower of Jesus.

Every time I speak or write in public, I want to allow for the possibility I am wrong about something or inaccurate, or that I simply don't know what I don't know, yet. This does not mean I lack faith, confidence, or preparedness—or an opinion, a position, or something I stand for. Good posture, as I define it, is to know what I know and how I've come to know it (tell those stories with humility), all the while seeking correction and conformity to a level of truthfulness I've yet to understand. Which is, specifically, all that is ever more trustworthy regarding God and people, and an increasingly expansive idea of place. For followers of Jesus, this, I believe, is living in accordance with the "walking humbly with God" part of Micah 6, and the reality of us as "walking contradictions" *and* the remarkable incremental transformation into Jesus' likeness written about in 2 Corinthians 3:18.

I have the benefit of being a student-follower of Jesus for over four decades. The things I've seen and heard living in community with fellow Christians and observing the church in America, the UK, and Europe, up close and personal, define glory and shame. I am no less implicated.

I've met selfless world-changers in the business of human flourishing in Jesus' name. I've heard truths trumpeted and profited from, only to be revealed as half-truths, lies, and the work of severely broken people at best, charlatans at worst. I've seen Christians give their money away and lay down their lives for justice for all—on the front lines of every global cause and emergency easily discerned as mattering to Jesus. And I've seen professing Christians, in America in particular, believe and perpetuate the most heinous and absurd lies, doubling down on them again and again. Hurting, even causing death to all that Jesus loves and values. These stories of light and darkness (now and over the centuries) are too many to be contained in books—though writers are giving it a go.

Whether anecdote, or the onion fully peeled, we the people (Christian or otherwise) have stark evidence of the reality of incremental transformation into the likeness of Jesus *and* colossal contradictions in thought and action. The first confirms that a loving Creator through Christ Jesus is keeping the promise of reconciliation and renewal. The latter is why the intervention was and continues to be necessary. This is also why so much of life, which includes writing and speaking in public, requires daily recalibration of where we've put our ultimate trust and confidence.

Of no less importance is having proximate understanding of one's spiritual, mental, and physical health—and tending to it as you are able. It should be obvious that these affect our ability to write and speak in public, positively and negatively. The fruit of our everyday lives tells us this is true. Sometimes a wound, trial, or pain leads to insight and wisdom. Or impatience, anger, resentment, and stress. All you need is one trip down Twitter/X lane to see the yin and yang on display 24/7.

With humility and understanding of one's health as the framework, this brings me to something very specific we can control, a friendly prescription: *Don't write or speak in public as if this gulf between glory and shame, health and unhealth isn't real.* We needn't be unnecessarily fearful of tarnishing Jesus' reputation. Superficially, it can appear that our public failures do just that. I'm familiar with James's tip regarding the folly of faith without evidence, and I agree. And, for the theo-techs, I agree with the sequence of justification to sanctification, with God in the driver's seat of both. Hebrews 6:4–6 comes to mind here too. Choose your exegesis, but no authentic Christian wants their bad behavior to hold Jesus up to contempt. I get it.

Take two steps to the side with me, though. Let's look at this from another angle. Jesus is, and has always been, held up to contempt—so much so that it led to his crucifixion. Though I would argue that for my generation the public verbal contempt is far more openly apparent than at any point in my life. People have no fear of publicly demeaning the person (or concept) of Jesus with hostility, glee, and freedom (and Christians are teeing up to do so with the frequency of a young Tiger Woods). If Jesus is the embodiment of God with us, an unfathomable mystery of the creative agency behind all that is and was and ever will be, then all the post-crucifixion contempt the world can sling at Jesus is the size of a dust mite on a proton. Cosmically, redemptively, all contempt has been dealt with, once for all.

Though it is nearly impossible for us to conceive of it, Jesus has moved on to another project—new humanity and new earth. Discerning and learning what this means existentially has increased our workload as writers and speakers. It is nothing less than the work of a lifetime. Granted, our idea and practice of the good news of the gospel includes the traditional, recurrent sin-and-salvation story. But this story cannot be limited to evangelism as it has been understood over the past several centuries—at least not for students of the work Jesus is actually up to. We are equally called (literally by Jesus) to be in the new-humanity and new-earth business, right now. Our storytelling will reflect this with understanding and faithfulness or risk failing to represent the whole story we are participating in.

Finally, there's that pesky word *truth*, and the Christian's use of it for all we believe and stand for about what constitutes reality. I made a minor case for the return of facts and truth in a form that is something other than the enlightenment's love affair with reason, or the bully's insistence on truth as my way or the highway.

Taking into account what I've shared about humility, my position on truth and the use of the word is this: Truth of the absolute kind exists. In the megastory of the physical cosmos with God as Alpha and Omega, I confess to know very little of this big-*T* truth personally. It is impossible for me to know, personally. I do not have the access or capacity.

I like to think that I have matured over the decades to do two things at once: hold to my inability to know what is true at all times and all places before God and humanity; and hold to my ability to know what has proved to be trustworthy about God, people, and the cosmos over time and in community with others (hoping to know the same). All that is trustworthy is what I feel confident in calling *truth.* Even though I am one small man among eight billion people, this knowledge-not-in-crisis is enough for me to sustain and enjoy a meaningful life. Yet, contrarily, it simply is not enough! I want more trustworthy truth. All I can get. When I write and speak, my hope is that my work takes a stand for these trustworthy truths *and* reveals my willingness to move in search of all that is newly trustworthy. I have this hope because of my trust in Jesus as the architect of redemption and new creation.

The final, best piece of advice I can pass on regarding the subject of this letter is to write and speak what you know to be trustworthy, proven over time, personally and in community with others—people of good will, like-minded and willing to challenge your assumptions and prejudices. Frame what you know as what you *best understand at this time.* If you have a proven, unwavering certainty (as I do with Jesus), then by all means share it with others with humility and respect for your audience. Avoid religious cliché as you would a swarm of mosquitoes; consider that many positions or opinions you hold are the possible result of privilege, untested and disconnected from the trustworthy reality of others; and by all means, Hippocratically, do no harm.

Instead, let your truthful, trustworthy storytelling, critiques, and even social media posts buttressed by righteous anger be generative, not degenerative. The Jesus summary of the law of love is contemporary to every generation in every situation. With this foundation, both dark and light truths can be generative, bearing fruit in the moment and for generations. It's the fruit that confirms the trustworthiness of any given word. Give it time.

ten

KNOWING WHEN IT'S TIME TO MOVE

To Those Considering a Big Change

from Andi

How can you know when it's time to leave a good thing behind?

Before it was ever time to do it, Chuck and I had many conversations about leaving our Art House home on the southwest edge of Nashville to move closer to the city. The subject arose from time to time as the years added up, and when it did, we were ambivalent, full of emotions equal to the meaning the house held for us. On the one hand, the house and property were a heavy weight, one we couldn't imagine carrying all the way through our lives. On the other hand, it had everything we needed for life and work, and we loved it intensely—every knob on every cupboard, every flower in the gardens. We'd created the place together, each in our own way, and poured ourselves into the life we'd been given there. It fit us like second skin and held a lot of our identity. We wondered who we'd be in another place—would we still feel like ourselves, would we still be ourselves?

131

But even so, we sometimes dreamed of being free; of lightening the load by moving to a place that was smaller, inexpensive to maintain, easy to manage, and just a home, not a recording studio, guesthouse, community gathering space, or anything else.

A year before we put the house up for sale, we decided to take a weekend to try out what it might be like to live closer to the city, able to walk to coffee shops, restaurants, and maybe even to work. We stayed in a hotel downtown and spent mornings in coffeehouses, one at Crema and one at Fido, sipping lattes, thinking, and writing. We drove through potential neighborhoods, touring one little house on a street where homes were selling the day they went on the market. We visited a studio on Music Row, walked up and down Twelfth Avenue South, browsed Holly Williams's store White's Mercantile, and savored late-afternoon appetizers at Epice, the Lebanese restaurant next door. On our second evening we met friends for dinner in East Nashville and told them what our weekend experiment was about. As good friends do, they listened with their hearts, asked great questions, and gave us their honest thoughts.

For me, some of the conversation about moving was spurred on by the fact that we'd been living inside of two family emergencies, sharing our home with loved ones who were in physical, mental, and emotional pain. As my mother-in-law recovered from an open-heart surgery that sent her into full-blown dementia, Sam was in the early stages of an extremely difficult divorce. He and the children needed sanctuary.

Out of necessity, Mom had made a quick decision to come to Nashville for heart surgery. Her plan was to return home to California afterward, but in her late seventies would that be possible? No one knew.

With a health emergency, you do the next right thing and figure the rest out later. So that's what we did. Before and after surgery she went back and forth between my sister-in-law's house and our house, two weeks in each place, getting more confused every time we packed her bags. Even with the aunts from California coming to help as they could, it was a lot to handle all at once, especially with Sam's family in so much pain.

I had a frozen-shoulder episode during this time and took to wearing a dish towel as a sling. Until I could get to an orthopedic doctor, it was the best I could do. It was impossible not to use my arm in the kitchen to chop, cook, stir pots, and pick up my little granddaughter, Brinsley. Comforting my grandkids was what I wanted to do most of all.

I was so often sad, angry, and full of grief over what was happening to the people I loved, especially the children. I couldn't sleep without Ambien. I looked for a therapist.

When Mom was around, I trailed her all day long. I feared her getting lost in our big house, which connected to the studio by a long hallway with painted concrete floors. In her confused state, it was not safe for her to wander. She'd already tripped on a rug and fallen. I feared it happening again, so I abandoned other work and stayed close.

I was an introvert with no time alone to recharge my batteries. We were sandwiched between the overwhelming needs of three generations, sometimes feeling the grace of being carried along, and at other times feeling crushed beneath the weight of it all. When one of our frequent houseguests called because the place she was supposed to stay burst a pipe and flooded, I was numb. On my worst days, the thought crossed my mind that if we didn't have this house, we wouldn't always be in the position to take people in. Caring for our family was my priority, the great need of the moment. I didn't have the energy for anyone else.

By the time we had our weekend getaway, I was aching for the ability to reengage my life and work, to do the things that ground me and make me, *me*. In order to accommodate all the extra, Chuck and I had rearranged our schedules, canceled things, and said "no thank you" to most any offer or request that wasn't absolutely necessary to making a living. In the beginning I tried to maintain the habits of a writing life, but each day had a mind of its own, and the hours of solitude necessary for writing slipped away. In response to my dehydrated and shriveled state of mind and heart, I fantasized a completely different life, one where our work happened away from home and we came back in the evenings to a cozy little house, just us.

Though we'd booked the getaway hotel for three nights, after the second night, Chuck woke up in the morning and said, "Honey, can we please go home?" He spoke what I was feeling. I was enjoying the time alone with my husband and the freedom to roam around the city, but I wanted to go home too. My soul had rejected every neighborhood we looked at and every house that wasn't ours. I grew quickly irritated with crowds, traffic, noise, and waiting in lines. All I could think of was going home to all that was ours.

I wanted to watch the perennial gardens I'd planted over the past two decades come to life one more time and listen to the birds and quiet. I wanted to be surrounded by things that mattered to me—the books and photographs that filled every room, the pantry wall in the kitchen with dates and names written in pencil to record our grandchildren's growth, and the mural our daughter, Molly, painted on the wall in her room when she was a teenager. I wanted my husband to have the perfect fit of his studio, and I wanted my small but beloved office, made beautiful only a few years earlier with a wraparound desk, floor-to-ceiling bookshelves, and a painted-blue wood floor. I thought of summer mornings and evenings in our screened-in porch, winter conversations in front of the fire, and my kitchen, designed and equipped for the hard work of cooking. And I wanted to plant the whimsical vegetable garden space that Chuck had been creating with master carpenter Richard Kapuga, our beloved friend who'd done every renovation and repair since 1990. It was an outdoor room so inspiring that even in its early stages total strangers stopped their cars to take pictures.

With all of this in our hearts, we got in the car and left the hotel, returning home to what we love. Before long, the acute stages of family emergency passed and everyone moved on to more permanent situations. Mom went to live with my sister-in-law and brother-in-law, Terri and Doug, and we provided respite care when they traveled or needed a break. As things returned to a more normal state, I found myself feeling more placed than ever, letting go of questions about the future and digging into life as I knew it right then.

The first morning alone, I went to my chair in the big room. I opened my tattered Bible, its front cover torn off, the pages crinkled and worn. I began reading and praying through psalms and other scriptures that were underlined and marked like a road map. I wrote in my journal; reveling in the peaceful quiet, my body relaxed.

Another day, I put on my Master Gardener T-shirt and Japanese gardening pants and went outside to clean up the gardens in preparation for early-spring growth. I'd been wearing those pants for twenty-one years and felt sturdy when I put them on, ready to tackle the dirty work of plant life and soil. As the days warmed up and spring continued to unfold, Chuck and I began planting the new vegetable garden. For a while, he became a genuine urban farmer, reclaiming long-forgotten edges and corners of our property to use for good—a potato patch where scrub brush had always been, fruit trees and berry bushes planted in places I'd never even thought of cultivating, a bean tepee for the grandchildren to grow green beans and play in. Every day we woke up to look for the wonders God had urged into being through another cycle of day and night.

Cooking for recording and songwriting sessions was often spur-of-the-moment, or just a simple invitation to come in the house and eat whatever we were eating. At the very least I kept the snack basket filled in the studio or baked muffins on tracking days. But when I had enough advance notice and it made sense to the project and to my schedule, I made a more concentrated effort to feed everyone. Especially when vocals were being recorded in the chapel space, right in the middle of our house.

Just then I was cooking for Joy Williams's sessions as Chuck produced her record. Joy and I are good friends, and I liked taking care of everyone when the sessions were long and daily. For lunches and dinners I made potato leek soup topped with sautéed asparagus, mushrooms, and prosciutto; spice-rubbed pork tenderloin tacos; quiche with asparagus, goat cheese, and bacon; and salads topped with the salmon we'd caught in Alaska's Kenai River the summer before.

As I figured out menus and worked in the kitchen, I realized in a fresh way how much I enjoyed contributing my own creativity to the recording experience. It met a real need, and when I had the time to do it well, it was satisfying work.

As much as I felt the pleasure of imagining and creating with food, I also enjoyed lingering over a meal in the midst of a workday. It was my opportunity to connect with everyone and get to know new people. With musician talk, my mind often wanders when the conversation turns to new gear and stories of previous recording sessions. It's an insider's language, born of expertise and shared experience. But around the table the topics are broader, more interesting to me. I love the mystery present at the table of hospitality. We all bring complex personal stories, and part of life's pleasure is to listen, learn, and share without having to untangle things for each other. My business was to feed and welcome, and when I did that, I felt most myself. If I connected with someone on a deeper level and made a new friend, my pleasure was doubled and I felt relationally richer, privileged to have such a life.

As I continued cooking, writing, meeting with people one-on-one, taking occasional speaking engagements, helping my family, and partnering with Chuck to make a place that was beautiful and comfortable for us and for others, I knew I was on the right track for the moment. There was much to do, and my friend Kate Harris gave me words that helped. In her book *Wonder Women: Navigating the Challenges of Motherhood, Career, and Identity*, she wrote about coherence, "It allows each aspect of my responsibility and effort, role and desire to flourish according to its distinct and diverse nature."[1]

Coherence rooted in my life under God holds every dimension

of my life together. Yet in all of these things there will be tensions, deep satisfactions followed by frustrations. The solitude necessary for writing would be trumped by the needs of family and others. The unending cycles of weeds and dirty dishes would make some days feel futile. When I couldn't get out of the driveway because of so many parked cars, I would bang my fist on the steering wheel and long for privacy. And Chuck and I together would grow weary of the demands and complexities of our life and once again talk and pray about a new, simplified chapter. Everyone experiences the tensions. Sometimes they're telling us something. Other times they pass.

Around that time, we heard Wendell Berry interviewed at a gathering in our city. In the same way his books do, he talked about life in a way that touched our longing to be more human in the best ways. His words about neighborliness, fidelity, belonging, and doing good work connected deeply. When he spoke of seeing our places as worthy of attention, affection, and care, it made sense of the pull Chuck and I always felt to stay even when we thought we should go, to cultivate and care for the place we loved, and to live fully where we were. Right then, we couldn't imagine doing that anywhere else. One year later, we knew it was time.

Chuck had been hired by Lipscomb University to oversee the commercial music program he'd created for them. He began as a consultant the previous year and was contracted to begin full-time as the director in the fall of 2015. After so many years of producing records and doing artist development on our property, he was excited about a new setting, and I was excited for him. To follow that path, we needed to downsize, cut our overhead, and live closer to the university.

As for me, I was almost sixty by then and officially exhausted from years of living in a radically open home. I was still ambivalent about leaving the place I loved so much but ready not to have my work defined by it. I was dreaming other dreams.

And finally, our children were in full support of our moving and that was important to us.

After months of getting the place ready to sell and beginning the process, a completely unexpected thing happened. The Reeves family, our dear friends who'd been instrumental in creating Art House Dallas, bought our home. And then our beloved mutual friends Nate and Cassie Tasker moved their family in to host and direct the work of Art House Nashville for another seven years. It was a beautiful grace.

The week before we moved, Chuck and I gathered with our children and grandchildren and some of our extended family. Sitting around the long table in the big room, we ate pizza on paper plates and told stories of all the years. I didn't cry until we turned on the disco ball and danced for the last time. And then I let the tears fall.

eleven

RETURNING TO A WRITING LIFE

To Those Who Want to Find Time to Write

from Andi

Boarding a plane from San Antonio to Nashville in January 2012, we were on our way home from a weekend at Laity Lodge, an ecumenical retreat center located on the banks of the Frio River in the Texas Hill Country. It is a favorite place for us: the purposeful and beautiful environment, the warmhearted hospitality, the thoughtful content of every retreat, and the view of an open sky on a starry, starry night. It will fill your soul.

Whether listening to or presenting as a speaker, floating around the river on inner tubes, or getting to know interesting people over walks and delicious meals, we've always come back to Nashville with a sense of direction and words for life.

On this trip, we'd been to Laity Lodge for a private retreat with the Chrysostom Society, a group of distinguished writers of Christian faith. Chuck contributed music—a wonderful concert on Sunday night—and I was privileged to go with him and be a fly on the wall, soaking up words and stories from a community of people I admire and from whom I have learned so much. There are younger writers in the group, but most who made it to the retreat that year had gray hair and aging frames—writers with a long history of publishing poetry, novels, essays, memoir, spiritual writing, and theology with a literary touch. Some of the writers were new to me, and they are a glad discovery, but others, like Eugene Peterson and Luci Shaw, have written some of the most underlined and important books in our library.

With the fullness of our Art House life, I was having a hard time finishing any writing I started, and I was frustrated. I couldn't stay at my desk long enough to develop and complete one piece. As I listened in at the gatherings and had conversations over meals, I found that no one had a perfect writing life. Some were university professors who wrote in the summertime and found it hard to remember what they were writing about after nine months of teaching. They longed for sabbaticals. Some had a patchwork of other jobs and kept their deadlines by writing at night, on the weekends, and in waiting rooms. Others were dealing with sorrow, failing bodies, and the changing world of publishing.

It was good for me to hear these things from people who'd been at it for a long time, who continued to write regardless of the challenges they faced. Through their faithfulness to the vocation of translating experience into words, imagination into story, and scholarship into beautiful writing, the world is blessed and my life is enriched.

During a Communion service in the great hall of the lodge a year before this retreat, Chuck and I had held each other and prayed for "more of this and less of that." We were asking for more times of refreshing, more trust, more joy, and less self-inflicted pressure and stress. But there are times—and we all have them—when we have to put our heads down, our hands to the plow, and press on for the duration. The best-laid plans fall apart, so we try again, hoping to get closer to what our longings are telling us.

Rearranging time, habits, and expectations is easier said than done. People's needs and requests can speak louder than the quiet beckoning of an unfinished page. What's more, people-care sparks my imagination in a unique way. I love creating in this arena, and I don't want to give up responding to need or imagining for the good of those I'm meant to love. But there is a dilemma: how to care for the people in our lives and get other creative work done too. This is an old and common struggle.

If it seems like growing older should naturally take care of some of the tension, there's no guarantee it will. Aging only complicates the issue. In families, once children grow up, relational responsibilities become even more complex. People tend to multiply, adding children-in-law and their families, grandchildren, nieces' and nephews' spouses and children, along with the possibility of families being spread geographically. And with friendships, the longer you live, the more people you know. There is always a worthy human need or want beckoning.

The Southern Festival of Books is one of my favorite yearly events in Nashville. It takes place in October when the weather is usually stunning. One year I heard bestselling author Ann Patchett speak. With good humor, she shared about the difficulty of getting work done during a year when she had overnight guests for roughly 250 days. That is not my life anymore, but it was then, and I felt an immediate kinship. When I thought about it later, I wondered how in the world she ever got to her writing with that many people around. I couldn't find it in my notes, but I thought I remembered her mentioning a hotel. Looking for clues, I found an article Ann wrote for the October 16, 2010, issue of the *Wall Street Journal* titled "Did I Kill *Gourmet* Magazine?" In the article she spoke of her years as a travel writer for *Gourmet* and the kindness they constantly showed her. She wrote, "And when I had a particularly endless stretch of house guests, I told Sertl [Bill Sertl, her editor at the magazine] I would like to check into a very fine hotel alone and not leave the premises for a week." I don't know if she was referencing the same timeframe as when I heard her speak, but the issue is the same. All writers, including famous ones, have a unique life to navigate. The call to people and the call to writing are not mutually exclusive. For most of us, they coexist in some form, and we have to find our way through, adjusting as we go.

Currently, I find my way with fewer people in the house and more solitude. In fact, most of our neighbors would not be able to imagine us in our previous setting, with people coming and going at all hours of the day and night. We have a small gate at the front door and when we're working, we keep it closed. Unthinkable at the Art House! Necessary now. Callings shift and change.

I'm not naïve enough to expect perfection, but I do need time. As any writer knows, you must show up regularly to get your work done. It must be given priority and long hours of concentration. I write best if I start first thing in the morning, which means pushing everything else aside. If there are dirty dishes in the kitchen, keep walking. Don't start a load of laundry. Resist the urge to restore order in the household. Go directly to the desk. I've been known to keep the Christmas tree up until late January. It takes time to undo what was so carefully put together in December. No matter. It will get done, just not now. To get to my office I walk past the scattered debris of our living and turn a blind eye. If I tend to it, I can easily get sucked in and lose the whole morning. So I tell myself, "Keep moving. Don't look to the right or to the left, and don't stop until you reach your desk."

Sitting with an open laptop or a legal pad and laboring over words and sentences requires solid blocks of time: hours, days, weeks, and years. Some writers use outlines, organizing the flow of their thoughts before beginning to write. I'm more apt to launch right in and find out what I'm writing about by writing.

I have a file on my Mac titled "Andi's Writing Ideas," which a good friend helped me create in an Excel spreadsheet. It keeps my thoughts in one place: ideas and topics, detailed notes, and the outlet they might be used for, whether essay, book, or talk. It is wonderfully helpful, and in the weeks and months when it's truly impossible to keep a writing schedule, it provides reassurance that I do have things to say and a pool of ideas to draw from.

Whatever kind of life we have, whether thick with children or friends in the house or with other work that pays the bills, the writer herself is the only one who can lay claim to the quiet practices that make for a writing life. Even if you have no current ability to write anything longer than a journal entry, stay faithful to that appointment. And make the reading of good books an enjoyable and necessary part of life. The prolific and much-loved author Madeleine L'Engle had three recommendations for writers: "Read, keep an honest journal, and write every day." Stephen King, in his wonderful book *On Writing*, wrote, "If you want to be a writer, you must do two things above all others: read a lot and write a lot. . . . Reading is the creative center of a writer's life."[1]

I know it can be hard to find the time for these things. Unless you really love them and can't live without them. Then you will always be looking for ways to feed the literary person inside you.

In the long-ago days when I was a mom with children at home, I found that piecing things together a little at a time is what worked. I brought a book for carpool lines and orthodontist appointments. I read in the last half hour before the kids came home from school, and later when they went to bed. Even now, I look for small moments of time. I read while the chicken is roasting or when the only relief from back pain is thirty minutes on the couch.

One year in my mom life, I decided to create a more focused time for study. It was a little like homeschooling my grown-up self in literature. A friend lent me a syllabus and textbook from a class he had loved in college. I bought a good notebook and pen and started with a reading from the textbook, moving on to Flannery O'Connor's *Mystery and Manners*. This was 1992. I wrote in the notebook: "First day of literature study interrupted by two phone calls. Wised up and turned on the answering machine. Studied from 9 to 12 with laundry in between."

There were only five days of notes spread out over nine days. The rest of the notebook is empty. That's all the "create your own class" my life could sustain in that season. The hours given to our family business, houseguests, food, volunteer work, kids, and home took time. Not to worry. Keep reading good books. Keep writing. Join book groups.

By the time our children were teenagers, we lived in the Art House. To carve out space for myself, I had Friday night coffee parties. I was the only guest! If the kids were out with friends or just doing their own thing, and Chuck was in the studio, I drank coffee for the caffeine boost and read to my heart's delight. I can see myself at the kitchen table, reading Anne Morrow Lindbergh's *Gift from the Sea* and copying significant passages in my journal. Another Friday, I put my feet up on the purple chenille couch and read *Like Water for Chocolate* in one large gulp, finishing at midnight. The next time, it was Henry James's *The Portrait of a Lady*, and then *Cry, the Beloved Country* by Alan Paton.

I looked forward to those evenings with the giddiness of a much-anticipated date, using the time to write letters and update my journal as well. Those lovely hours fed me as a reader and a writer. I didn't know the writer in me would ever develop beyond my journals. I was just doing what I loved, creating space to nourish something in me that felt as necessary as breathing.

Even during the long years of my seminary studies when I read stacks of theology books during the day, I still read at night, but the books were different. They were stories. I needed the pure enjoyment of fiction and memoir, and the good food of literary writing.

These days I do most of my reading somewhere in the daytime hours when my eyes and my brain are not as tired. It doesn't matter when you read, only that you do. Reading and writing are companions. The pleasure of words and stories taken in nourishes the writing that goes out.

Several of our bookshelves are filled with books about writers and writing. Anne Lamott's *Bird by Bird*, Dani Shapiro's *Still Writing*, Donald Hall's *Life Work*, *The Writing Life* by Annie Dillard, and *The*

Writer on Her Work edited by Janet Sternburg—to name a few—are instructive, insightful, and inspiring. As with any vocation, it helps to hear from others who do what you do or what you dream of doing. I've spent a lot of time around musicians and songwriters whose creative work takes years of disciplined labor but is often done communally. Writing essays and books, on the other hand, is solitary work. Reading about other people's writing lives helps me stay focused. I'm particularly interested in hearing how writers steward the many dimensions of their responsibilities. One of my friends is a pastor, father, and author. Another is a mother of young children and a novelist. Everyone's lives are messy with overlap. No neat and tidy boxes.

In a book published in 1994, *Parting the Curtains: Interviews with Southern Writers*, Doris Betts was asked, "What would be your ideal writing day?" She answered, "I really have never had one. . . . Well, I was going to say it would begin with everybody waiting on me instead of the other way around." Kaye Gibbons answered the question "Do you usually write every day?" in this way: "Usually I write every day while Mary naps." These very human answers are a good reminder that few people write in an ivory-tower environment. Those who create a body of work over a lifetime keep coming back to the writer's desk regardless of the obstacles. They write because it's who they are.

This is the most important thing. Write because you have the urge to write, the need to write, because you can't *not* write. Do it for love. Think of the journals you've filled, the books you've loved, the half-written essays on your computer, or the sentences and paragraphs that might be a book someday if you could only believe it matters.

In my early forties, when Molly was in college and Sam was still in high school, I began to think about calling. What does it mean? Who is it for? In the family-farm nature of our life, I had a long habit of taking on all kinds of miscellaneous jobs without thinking. Sometimes it was necessary. Other times, not so much. Need an errand run? I'll do it. Somebody to do the bookkeeping? Okay. Thank-you notes and paperwork now that we have Art House? Let me squeeze that in. Saying yes to everything and no to nothing was not a wise way to live.

I was looking for a better way when I went with my friend Barbara to a class that psychologist Dr. Bruce McCurdy was just developing. The class was an exercise designed to help us understand and name what God had placed inside us to be and do and care about. We took personality tests. We answered questions about what settings we preferred to be in, what tools we liked to use, what fields of knowledge we already had, and what we would like to pursue. It wasn't about finding one magical thing that poked its head out. But it was about narrowing. What matters most?

In the process of working through the materials, I thought about being a bookish girl and a bookish woman. I thought of the coffee parties, the journals, my hunger for learning, and I realized that writing was there all along. It was there when I was a little girl and a teenager and a grown woman. It is one of the deeper, longer stories of my life, always there. That's when I began to trust that God had created me with gifts and ways of being. Giving those things their proper place was a part of following Jesus.

Shortly after the class was finished, Chuck and I took a leap of faith and hired an entertainment business management team to do some of what I had been doing and more. When a truck came and carted away boxes of paperwork from my office, I stood at the Art House kitchen door and watched with tears streaming down my face. In the whole scheme of years from then to now, it was temporary. We would hire out the work, then bring it back and do it mom-and-pop style again and again. But that day was a turning point.

I walked back through the house to my office, put up a bulletin board, cleared the desk of anything unrelated to writing and books, and began to listen to the ideas and questions that had been rolling around in my head for a while. I wrote a few sentences on one day, a paragraph on another. I researched. Pages added up. I paused for our children's weddings. I paused when we had houseguests. I paused when Chuck and I moved to Saint Louis for a semester of school. I paused when there were grandchildren to care for and large Art House events to host. But there has always been a returning.

Not long ago I roamed the house just before bed, stopping by my office to turn off a lamp. In the soft light I stood in the doorway and looked at the wall of books on one side of the room and my desk with pages of writing printed out on the other. Standing there, I was overwhelmed with the deepest knowing: all of this is a gift of love, a blessing of the Lord. I walked away with tears in my eyes and no words to describe it to Chuck when I reached the bedroom.

On one of those bookshelves there's a small black-and-white photograph of my sister Paula and me when she was eight and I was three. Our parents were still together. I know the stories. Paula and me hiding in our room. Mom screaming for Paula to get help from the neighbors. Mom wearing dark glasses to work when she had a black eye. My sister remembers me as invisible back then, quiet to the point of not being noticed, always looking down. Part of the wonder as I stood in my office doorway, the bookshelves almost glowing their message, is that this same little girl, now a woman in the latter half of her sixties, has been given a life filled with words: books, conversations, literary friendships, writing.

Not everyone wants to live in words, but some of us do. We are made for it. It is our solace and our joy. If this is you, dear reader, pray and write. Write and pray. Return to it all the days of your life. Together, let's be intentional in the daily process of growing as a writer. Let's narrow our focus, care for our family and friends, and get our work done. One sentence, one paragraph at a time.

twelve

DANGLING OVER THE CLIFF AND OTHER DANGERS

To the Sick and Suffering

from Charlie

It's not like I knew my life was headed for cataclysmic change. Monday, October 24 was a morning like any other morning in 2016. Teach a 9:00 a.m. class at Lipscomb University, then work out for an hour or two. Fitness and nutrition had become part of my identity. I was sixty years old and in the best shape of my adult life. I felt great. Which is why I was so surprised to wake up with a headache.

I didn't even bother taking ibuprofen. In an hour the headache would be gone. It wasn't. It stayed with me all day and night at precisely the same intensity. With each passing day, the pain remained the same. Very intense. Highly irritating. No variation. A rectangle in the center of my forehead.

On the morning of November 4, things got worse. I felt so bad

I couldn't get out of bed. I canceled my cardio-and-weights session. New symptoms had appeared. My head pulsed loud and unrelenting. The pounding caused my eyes to jump in rhythm. I was having something akin to a power brownout in my left ear. Like a flickering light, it was shutting on and off. Specific sound frequencies bothered me. My pulse spiked at random. I had a full-body, micro-trembling feeling as if I were vibrating. My face was a minefield of twitches firing off. Spasms moved up and down my legs. My whole body felt like it wanted to steer left all the time. Like leaning into a curve. I was fatigued and mentally off. When I wasn't thinking unclearly, I wasn't thinking at all. I kept saying, "I'm not right." Through it all, the headache remained. Not headaches. All one headache, all the time.

I tried to keep working, willing myself to remain positive around students and colleagues at Lipscomb University, where I was the director of the School of Music. Our family doctor referred me to a neurologist. I was thoroughly questioned, poked, and scanned. I consulted with several additional specialists, including an Epstein-Barr virus expert at the National Institutes of Health. The only bit of quantitative data they could find was white blood cells and protein in my spinal fluid and elevated norepinephrine. As the neurologist flatly said, "I know you have something, and it is vexing to me."

Though I was eventually given pain medication (after two months), it had little to no effect on the headache. In some ways, the drugs and accompanying brain fog made it worse. It's hard to teach or meet with prospective students and their parents when you can't put sentences together.

After 120 days of a single intractable headache, daily, unnerving passages of crazy had become my new norm. A ten on the headache scale is a truly mind-bending experience. My mouth pushed out grunts in half notes, largo tempo. I thought I was dying. I begged God to make it stop.

On March 8, 2017, Andi and I flew to Mayo Clinic in Scottsdale, Arizona. I had a three-and-a-half-hour consultation with an integrative medicine specialist. Unlike every other doctor I had seen, this one was willing to venture a diagnosis. My central nervous system had been severely compromised. The reason I felt like I was coming apart . . . is that I was.

He explained that the sympathetic component of my fight-or-flight response was stuck "on"—something called dysautonomia or autonomic nervous system dysfunction. He put it like this: "You're hypervigilant—always alert for danger. Your brain and central nervous system are refusing to go into rest mode. It thinks there's a saber-toothed tiger in the room with you—all the time, everywhere."

He talked about something called central sensitization, a condition of the nervous system associated with the development and mainte-nance of chronic pain. When central sensitization occurs, the nervous system goes through a process called "windup" and gets regulated in a persistent state of high reactivity. This is not tissue related. The brain is the genesis of the headache pain based solely on past trauma and past and present stress triggers. This diagnosis also explained my other symptoms, including ear issues (hyperacusis). As with PTSD, my brain was creating sound sensitivities that had nothing to do with my ears. They were real and painful (and selective) sensitivities, but they were not tissue related.

The doctor asked if I needed to work. Could I quit my job at Lipscomb University or take a leave of absence? No, I don't need to work, though I *do* need to because I'm the head of the School of Music. He asked, "Do you want to get better?"

This doctor read me like a book. He explained how my lifetime of mystery illnesses, recurrences of what I thought was Epstein-Barr virus, the one-hundred-day headache I'd had several years back, ver-tigo, anxiety attacks, working till I was sick, then going to bed for a week just so I could begin the cycle again—all of these were storylines in a single drama. Now, through some perfect storm of triggers, I was experiencing the mother of all manifestations of this one overarching illness, a complete central nervous system meltdown. My body had kept the score, and I was losing. A week in bed wasn't going to fix me this time. I'd used up all the resilience allotted to me.

The doctor diagrammed a multifaceted plan for recovery. This included antidepressants; alternative therapies such as acupuncture, massage, biofeedback, EMDR, and Reiki; dietary supplements; mindfulness; and breathing exercises. My workout regimen would have to change. Cardio and weights, always pushing through pain to higher goals, was hurting and not helping. Walking would do just fine. He stressed the importance of family, talk therapy, spiritual life, nutrition, sleep, and in general a life made of more than work. "Do you have a hobby or a pet?" he asked, adding, "If not, perhaps you could get one or more."

All in all, I would have to slow down the tempo, concentrate on these forms of self-care, family, and community, and, in a phrase, "unlearn my pain."

I came back to Nashville grateful and hopeful that my headache and accompanying symptoms would one day be gone. I took a leave of absence from the university and worked my new self-care program, and for several months the headache was less severe, and some of the accompanying symptoms disappeared. Things were looking up. Yet, even with such good progress, I had no way of predicting the dark tunnel that lay ahead.

During the worst of this illness, I would wake up each day more fearful than the next. I kept saying, "It's as if my life force is leaving me." Like in a science-fiction thriller when the monster sucks the life out of its victim and you see a stream of light leaving the body. So this is it? So this is how it all ends? I was gripped with fear that it was true, that I would, with no warning, drop to the floor, gone. I was terrified of sudden death, a death so unexpected there would be no time to gather the family, profess love, make amends, say how proud I am of the grown children and grandchildren, and embrace Andi one last time with gratitude for the life we've made together. There would be no time for prayers, my favorite Bible passages, or a chorus of "Amazing Grace." In short, a death I could not control.

I'm supposed to believe that the clock on eternal life started ticking the second I was in the company of Jesus as his disciple. (This is basic Christian doctrine.) As the hymn says, "No guilt in life, no fear in death. This is the power of Christ in me. From life's first cry to final breath, Jesus commands my destiny."[1] This is what I believe. Death, from life to life.

Years before on December 5, 1992, I was at Biola University in Southern California doing a typical sound check ahead of the concert I'd be performing that evening. "Can you turn me up in the monitors?" "Is your guitar buzzing onstage?" The concert never happened. I received a call that my father had collapsed and died on the living room floor. Sudden death.

Twenty-five years later, in the grip of chronic illness, my greatest fear was nothing more than my deepest pain. The body keeps the score. No passage of time, no hymn or doctrine, has been able to take away the pain of my dad's death. I simply cannot get over it. Relationships that matter most never lose their hunger for most of what really matters. A glimpse of approval, forgiving words, long embraces, kisses on the forehead, confessions and amends, laughter, and saying long good-byes. Maybe that's it; maybe I'm stuck in a long good-bye.

My position at Lipscomb University had begun in 2014, when I had been hired as a consultant to create a contemporary music curriculum. The idea was for me to do a deep dive into what's given me a sustainable career for four decades, and then turn the findings into a bachelor's degree in music (with the much-needed help of two academics, Donna King and Dr. Sally Reid). I thrive doing this kind of short-term intensive analysis and problem-solving. The consultancy led to becoming the director of the new program, and eventually the director of the entire School of Music, and the overseer of a new Lipscomb property, the Sound Emporium Studios.

While I loved teaching the students and the friendship of a few openhearted colleagues, the work put me face-to-face with an unforeseen nemesis: institutional bureaucracy. After a career of being in charge creatively and financially, I was now at the mercy of ever-shifting boundaries, budgets, and plans. By October 2015, I was sick with what I thought to be an Epstein-Barr virus flare-up. I resigned my position and then quickly took it back when the dean graciously reshaped my commitments.

My new position also, finally, prompted Andi and me to leave the Art House property for a lovely urban house a mile from the university. We imagined a quieter, simpler life. My work aside, I saw the move as a chance for Andi to realign with her writing and recover from decades of hospitality work. Her calling to hospitality is genuine, and she was a creative, warmhearted host to thousands of people who came through our home. Yet both of us had peaked from *too-muchness*. We longed for a private home where we could enter a new season of life and grow closer as a couple. It didn't happen. Leadership at a university produced the opposite result. Looking back now, I can see that Andi and I had little time to reflect on, even grieve over, our move from the Art House, a home God used in remarkable ways. We'd traded a great meaning-maker for a house. We were both unhappy and too often saw only the negative in circumstance and each other. This was not us. We were in trouble.

In our new neighborhood, there's an alley separating our house from the back of our neighbor's. Shortly after moving in, I was disappointed to find out that our back neighbor was always yelling. Again, not the peace we hoped for. But worse than that, he would go into fits of rage, swearing and belittling his wife and children. All of this happened in their open garage or in the alley, right outside our bedroom window. There was no possible way not to hear it. His anger and screaming voice were terrorizing. Yes, to his poor family, but to me too. I felt like it was happening to me.

As part of my headache therapy in 2017, I began a treatment known as EMDR, or eye movement desensitization and reprocessing. It was initially designed to alleviate the distress associated with traumatic memories and is often prescribed for people with PTSD. EMDR helps the brain unlearn its pain, allowing for it to activate its natural healing ability. This is all about the science of brain plasticity.

There's a landmark study that was sponsored by Kaiser (a healthcare giant) and the US Centers for Disease Control and Prevention. It's called the adverse childhood experiences study, often referred to as ACEs. There are ten types of childhood trauma measured in the ACE study. Five are personal: physical abuse, verbal abuse, sexual abuse, physical neglect, and emotional neglect. Five are related to family: an alcoholic parent (any alcohol or drug abuse), domestic violence against the mother, a family member in jail, a family member diagnosed with a mental illness, and the absence of a parent through divorce, death, or abandonment. There are, of course, many other types of childhood and adult trauma. These ten were the dominant ones in this particular study of childhood trauma. For each trauma you've experienced, you receive a point, ten being the highest.[2]

The study found a stunning link between childhood trauma and chronic diseases, as well as social and emotional problems.[3] In short, toxic stress and trauma change a child's developing brain. It can turn your mind into a hypervigilance factory. It can make you think you're not alive unless you're doing everything in your power to keep yourself safe and moving forward.

Though my ACEs are quite high, there's been a positive flipside for me. My resilience scores are even higher. It's evidence of why I didn't meet the mother of all central nervous system crashes sooner. It was in me, ready to blow anytime, and often leaking out, but my chronic resilience was keeping it from entirely incapacitating me.

Through EMDR therapy I faced my deepest and darkest traumas, including early childhood sexual abuse. I located my triggers. While I received some immediate physical relief, it mostly wrecked me and made me crazier than I've ever been. I grieved things I had never thoroughly grieved or given myself license to. I found my anger and lashed out, casting blame on Andi and others. Day after day I felt a deep, unrelenting sadness. And for the first time in my life, I let myself feel the full weight of my child/teenager self. I allowed myself to fail, to not be strong. I faced the unfiltered me—which, as it turned out, was not my chilled-out, everything-is-cool persona. I found the troubled, hurt, and angry child, teenager, and young adult who turned his head from trauma, ran as fast as he could, tried to mute the noise through drug and alcohol abuse (then musical achievement), and failed to grieve any of it for more than a day. I had never learned to occupy my pain and suffering. It was not our family way. Bad things happen. You move on.

Much has been made of our marriage at various times over the past few decades. By us and by others. Together since fifteen, married at eighteen and nineteen. Teenage romance and still married after forty-eight years? A miracle! That sort of thing. Mythological in proportion. The whole truth? Less triumphant.

Andi and I lived through things between the ages of fifteen and twenty-five that have always needed acknowledgment and grieving. That's not counting what we lived through separately before then. Sure, we had talked about some of it. We'd been to therapists and filled up notebooks in recovery groups. The unexpected call to follow Jesus in the early 1980s had immediate and immeasurable positive effects on our lives. We were swept up in the mercy and forgiveness of God, and so very grateful. Spending any more time going back seemed like an insult to the whole concept of redemption and new humanity in Christ. Wasn't Jesus going to restore the years the locusts had eaten?

Perhaps so. But if you've got stories living in your brain that you fear thinking about for even one second, the pest of trauma is still crunching away at your insides. So it was with me. Though I was, as the hymn proclaims, in "the everlasting arms" of Jesus, I was no less in need of a savior. More than ever. More than when I first believed. And I wasn't alone. What was happening to me was happening to Andi. For better or for worse—mostly worse. I was processing. Communicating poorly. Disassociating. In phenomenal headache pain.

And because of this, we were not unlike a couple who suffers tragedy, something so weighty they can't recover personally and so the marriage can't either. For a moment, we dangled over that cliff.

It was the worst possible time to have our unity divided. I was a child in a sixty-year-old man's body. Some portion of every day was spent wrecked and in tears. My mother was dying in a memory care facility. Richard Kapuga, an essential person in our lives and in the creation of Art House and our recording studios, had died. Chris Cornell, an artist I'd produced for the film soundtrack to *12 Years a Slave*, took his own life. It seemed that everything had gone dark, yet it hadn't. There was light.

At just the right time, our friends circled around us, and a couples therapist helped us talk. We learned to begin every sentence with "What I make up about you is . . ." In other words, what I'm about to say is what I feel and perceive; it may or may not be accurate; my heart and mind are open to discuss, listen, and process together. A handy device. A way of being.

At just the right time we found each other again. Faith, hope, and love would have the final word. Not because they were a bright, happy bow on our recovery and escape from completely unraveling—no bright red bows were or are present. Faith, hope, and love delivered in the end because they were there in the beginning—the first trustworthy words that wooed, inspired, and formed us as a young couple in the "everlasting arms of Jesus." We found each other in the continuity of our redemptive story and in the reality of our brokenness and collective trauma. We found the land of *nowhere-left-to-run* and made our dwelling. Which is, all of it, every bit the Jesus story. After fifty-plus years together, we still had much to learn. Still do.

Part of my brokenness is my perceived need to always be creating the world I want to live in. Emphasis not on the concept but on the word *always*. My heart and head can get way out in front of my body. My imagination has a capacity that my body does not, and it is the body that calls a stop when needed. Correctly, it knows it needs rest. My imagination didn't get the memo. It has taken a lifetime to see this and let myself off the hook, to make peace with my limitations as one small, broken person, and not feel a failure for leaving a great deal of the imagined uncreated. It's been essential for me to come to terms with how I came to see imagining and creating as a solution to my human condition. A very long time ago, as a child, I learned that imaginary play and creation made me feel safe and good about myself. Once people outside my immediate family began to reward me for this behavior, I was dependent on it. You may relate to this or have your own version of it.

There is a paradox at work in me and around me. Though I cannot have and execute what I used to call *big ideas* (e.g., creating companies and academic programs), I am having the most productive period of my entire artistic career. Call it the Van Gogh effect (because of his famously productive two-year period) or some other clever description. However one names it, I am imagining and creating hundreds of musical compositions, art pieces, and stories, while creating little to no bad, unhealthy stress. And I'm doing it with a 24/7 headache.

The survivor in me used to think that avoiding pain and suffering was essential. To face the reality of it was to risk being derailed and spun off the fast track. For example, I might see an email or a box of old photos, could be anything, and think: *I can't look at that right now. I don't have time to be undone, crying and convulsing for an hour.* Or I would ignore physical problems such as dizziness, trembling, and ear brownouts because music projects needed to be completed. Failing was not an option . . . yet.

The new, hopeful, more informed and honest me learned that facing my pain and suffering was essential and the only road forward to good health. I would have to unlearn my pain in order to one day be pain-free—which was, naturally, my goal. I knew this would take prioritizing my health, committing to different healing modalities, old and new. At first I thought, on the outset, it would take a year to turn this thing around. As I write this, I'm well past six years. The number of doctors and specialists I've seen, tests I've endured, drugs I've taken, and alternative medicines and methods I've tried would take up a thirty-page letter just to outline them. It really is phenomenal. If you suffer, or have suffered, chronic pain, you know this story, don't you? Still, I delight in hearing when another fellow sufferer is healed or finds the magic fix and all is made right. Unfortunately, I haven't found it yet, or it hasn't found me. Even so, prayers, old and new, are being answered.

Because I believe that prayer is always an efficacious conversation with God, I pray for healing in general, and specifically for the headache. Prayer isn't a request hotline though—like when I was a kid calling the local radio station to play a favorite song. If I could get a KOBO DJ to answer, I knew they'd take my request and play "Sweet Caroline." I'm confident God is picking up the phone and listening. That unique mix of what God's will is and the timing for it, though, is out of my hands.

Hundreds of loving people have prayed and continue to pray for my wellness and healing. Prayers are being answered. But not always in the exact form we've requested, such as being headache-free. If the prayer is *Lord, in your mercy, heal Charlie*, then efficacy is underway. I am being healed of sickness and the lifetime effects of sin and circumstance. Believe me, I want this headache gone, but I would never go back to the pre-headache me. Keep praying.

A few years back, I wrote a short piece about my illness for our blog. I cringe a bit in recalling some of my proactive language. I was trying to take control of the illness and its triggers, telling my readers "I was taking down names, hunting the enemies, staring them down, and making some demand of surrender." Oh my. Aspirational language building up oneself or others is not wrong. It is part of every competitive sport. But chronic pain, sickness, and suffering is not sport, is it? In reality, for this man, autonomous control never leads to peace (and believe me, my internal engine thinks it does). Cooperating with what Jesus has in mind does not begin with a battle plan. It requires a shift in thinking, a new posture, eyes to see, that sort of thing—which is almost always a long reveal and not sudden enlightenment and embodiment (though the latter does happen).

Jesus tells us not to expect the peace he gives to be anything like what the world gives (John 14:27). The peace on offer is not the absence of conflict, suffering, injury, or the promise that tears will not flow every time I think of my father or plummet into a pain volcano. It is the peace that persists despite the pain, headache or otherwise. The peace of Jesus is the assurance of shalom—the recovery of wholeness and irreversible well-being. A peace in motion—promised, yes, but for now incomplete and proximate.

Which leads to acknowledging the Christian realist in me. The man committed to the hope of new humanity and earth, currently still loosely tethered to the old. Cooperating with the plan with headache in hand. Living in the fullness of reality.

The biggest shift in my approach to life is allowing myself to fail, to be embarrassed, misunderstood. I still get quite angry at being disrespected—there's a generational trauma story there you'll have to look for elsewhere. But in general, I've adjusted to being weak and unreliable. Ten years ago I could never conceive of such a thing. Today, it is pure freedom, and a slice of good-health pie that exists in spite of the headache and other neurological symptoms, like internal trembling. I smile at the memory of telling a neighbor that I was no longer trustworthy—that I might say I would do something for the neighborhood HOA and then back out, and basically fail. I'm not sure she believed what I was telling her. It's difficult for me to comprehend, too, that I would tell someone, "I'm sorry, I can't do this," and then go take a nap and not be worried about their opinion of me. Being limited has somehow opened up a new world of seemingly limitless possibilities (even if I'm the only one experiencing them).

In case my words appear too rosy or laissez-faire, let me be clear about something. I have days when I despair unto death. I say things like "I just don't know how much longer I can take this." I have not experienced suicidal ideation, but I understand a level of pain and suffering that inspires the question of how I will continue on. I do not keep this to myself; I tell others as I feel led to. It is what is real.

In addition to learning to say no, I have gathered to myself a few practices or helps. They change and evolve as needed. But having them at hand is a kind of comfort. I don't mention them to be prescriptive but to describe what is real and helpful to me at this time. Speaking of time, it figures significantly into my ad hoc wellness program.

As much as possible, I do not live by the clock, particularly as it has to do with sleep. As per sleep experts' suggestions, I go to sleep at generally the same time each night, usually by 11 p.m. I sleep as long as is needed. Might be till 6:00 a.m. or 10:30 a.m. I don't like the later time, but I give myself grace for it, saying to myself, *I guess I needed it.* This means I can't schedule anything early. Of course, occasionally, there's a doctor's appointment that has to be at 8:30 a.m. and I roll with it. I never plan anything, though, especially not talking to or meeting anyone, before 11:00 a.m.

I also divide my labor into blocks of time and remain open to a nap every day as needed. Anything that requires writing I do first after the coffee is made and the prayers are said. After forty-plus decades as a follower of Christ and a participant in evolving Christian culture, I yield to no one's new and definitive ideas about quiet time and devotions. Sorry. *Quiet time* and *devotions* are not in my vocabulary—though I suspect I experience them often. I pray because I want to begin talking to the Creator about the day to come, and to express thanks for another day of grace and possibility. I pray Matthew 6:9–13, the Lord's Prayer, and the "Confession of Sin" from the Book of Common Prayer. I pray for my family members by name and anything else that comes to mind. Then I get to work. Prayer and thanks are integrated into the rest of the day. Seamlessly devoted, I hope.

Once fatigue begins to bloom and the headache starts shouting, I create a change of venue. Eat, go for a walk, take an early nap—in the summer we swim at the YMCA. After a bit, if I do start working again, I tackle something that doesn't require the level of concentration writing does. Household chores, artwork of some kind, or music, which is akin to breathing for me at this point in life. By 4:00 p.m., I'm usually out of gas. If I haven't napped, I'll do another change of venue, lie down, watch some YouTube fishing videos, and fall asleep for an hour. This is my workable, sustainable day. On most days I can do this and live the life in front of me.

After taking many drugs over the past six years (including every migraine medication you've ever seen advertised), I have, with my doctor, weaned off all but the essentials. I want to be present in every moment and clearheaded. Even so, each day there are times when the pain is just too debilitating and I crave relief. While I do have my emergency meds, I find it just as effective in the short run to use my brain distractions. In my case, because of the headache I use two TheraICE neoprene cold caps that I keep in the refrigerator or freezer. They interrupt the pain by putting the attention on the cold gripping my head, not the headache. Similarly, I use a TENS unit on my forehead and another on my neck, flooding the pain zone with electrical impulses. Not only is there relief during the distraction, but for twenty minutes to an hour after as well. Neither of these is a cure, but they do, in a sense, buy me time by lowering the severity of pain or simply giving my brain something to do other than telling me how much trouble I'm in—*You know you have a really bad headache; you should do something about it.* Thanks, I hadn't noticed.

Depending on the level of pain, I might use these helps at intervals throughout the day. Occasionally, days will pass and I realize, wow, I haven't used them at all. Having the ability to control the pain, even in small doses, is comforting and gives me some agency over my disorder.

Regular, weekly physical therapy and chiropractic sessions function in the same way.

As I mentioned earlier, for trauma-related illness, I found EMDR therapy essential. Much later in my journey I began receiving ketamine infusions. While these have not proved to demonstrably reduce my headache, they have had healing effect—especially when they are guided by a licensed therapist. As a Christian, these treatments worked to center me afresh in Christ and give me perspective, both in positivity and in my place in God's vast creation. In one visit, the therapist transcribed me saying: "I am but one small pebble in the stream, but I am wet." In Christ, in perspective, and grateful.

Now, let me state the obvious. I have the freedom to control my time and therapy in this way. I work from home and have the resources to give to this care. Living with chronic sickness and suffering is all-consuming. It is hard work recovering something of the good you once knew, or maintaining any semblance of a life you love or aspire to. We all do the best we can with what we have. And hopefully, we don't do it alone.

Andi is essential to my health (as is my whole family). Not only is Andi in it with me and for me at every turn, but her presence, her person, our long history of ascents and descents mean everything to me. No one knows us like we know each other. Being known by her (especially the unfiltered me) produces a peace that continually feeds my well-being. If you ever wonder what the unique fruit of a long marriage or relationship is, I can answer that. It is the freedom to be yourself unedited and broken, sick and suffering, and not rejected. It is unconditional love. The love we Christians profess is paramount to what we receive and give as followers of Jesus.

I was never one to give much credence to any merger of positivity and Christianity, vis-à-vis prosperity gospel. Pain and suffering has taught me the importance of positivity, though. You already know I like keeping it real, as in reality as I best understand it. Keeping it positive, as in hopeful, curious, and ready for the appearance of good, is just as important. Especially so while living with chronic pain and sickness.

I exercise the freedom to quietly excuse myself from (or flee) negative people putting (here comes the 1970s Californian in me) *negative energy out into the world.* Positive people, comfortable in their own skin, real about life's trials, but hopeful, are good medicine. Pain and suffering (in all their miserable forms) are real, and most often the causes are not easily explained, or explained away.

If a professing Christian ever tells you that your suffering is nothing compared to what Christ suffered on the cross, two things are true at once. One, yes, there's no comparison in the grand, cosmic sense. And two, the comparison is a false equivalence and of no value to you or any person suffering from chronic pain or illness. Flee from such a person, correct them, or disregard their banal cliches with a smile. Jesus died on the cross once for all, for all sin and all decay leading to death. No other martyrs or saviors needed. Job fulfilled.

Your job is to be you, and to remember that you're a person deeply loved, in pain, who is suffering. If Jesus is who he says he is, then he has always seen you in the fullness of who you are and what has, and will, happen to you in a lifetime. He knows you and your pain. That is not a fix or meant to be, but an assurance that you are not unknown or alone.

In our time, on our dime, everything is proximate except the promise that it will not always be this way. Some days that's a help. Some days the promise fails to penetrate. Nothing to fix here. No performance needed. Just be. But if at all possible, be in communion with others who do and will love you—who will be your help and something of the promise in the here and now. They may not be suffering the same pain and sickness as you, but if they are honest, openhanded, and openhearted, they will take you seriously and treat you with kindness. If you are all with Jesus in Spirit and mission, then you enjoy a mutual trust in the coming crescendo of *setting all things right*. Newness on its way, ETA unannounced. But in faith, fully confident in the plan and in the One executing it.

Until then, love and be loved; don't get too lonely, tired, or hungry; pray and be prayed for; accept the reality that you don't have it all figured out and don't need to; give yourself the freedom to not be okay, to fail even. Surround yourself with positive, loving people; avoid the negative and the religious people-fixers; find and use your helps and change them up as often as you like. And, by all means, take as many naps as you need. I pray you dream as one well and greatly loved.

thirteen

THE KNOT THAT HOLDS

To Those on the Long Road of Marriage

from Andi

In the late summer of 2017, Chuck and I sat across from a marriage counselor trying to sort out the tangles of our then forty-two years together. Therapy was not new to us, but this kind was different. It was painful, a chisel cracking through marble. We dreaded going.

From a romance that began in high school to the changing landscape of later life, there were long patterns of behavior to wade through, different ways we'd each experienced the same history, perennial issues and resentments that sizzled under the surface, and all kinds of beauty and goodness getting lost that needed remembering.

Our therapist said we were developmentally on task for a couple in their early sixties—assessing our lives, correcting mistakes, and making conscious decisions about what we wanted our lives to look like moving forward. It was good to know that something was normal because everything else was hard to make sense of. We didn't feel like ourselves and hadn't for some time. When I answered the assessment questions before our first meeting, I felt like a stranger in my own skin. I wouldn't have responded in the same way even a few months earlier.

Have you ever been in that place, dear reader? Whether a year into your marriage, or five years, or forty, where you don't feel like yourselves? Maybe you step on a land mine, a trigger. In a flash, you are in a cycle of defensiveness or blaming you can't escape. You don't even know how you got there. Too many words are spent, or maybe not enough words, but you both walk away wounded. It takes days to recover. Or perhaps you're inside a circumstance that is so beyond your understanding that, as it plays out, you look at each other and wonder—who are these people?

As Chuck has described so beautifully in his letter to the sick and suffering, his illness kicked off a strange season in our long life together. Every painful thing we'd ever been through, whether separately grieved or talked about a million times with no resolve, came busting out in the crisis of his suffering.

At first he was withdrawn, barely communicating except for getting-through-the-day kinds of things. I felt shut out and alone, having to guess what was happening inside him. I later understood that severe physical and emotional pain changes us and makes us desperate. We're just trying to get through the next ten minutes, the next hour.

Historically, though, on and off through the decades of our life together, we've both had times of withdrawing. Whether unable or unwilling to name what was going on inside us, we left the other person guessing. You may be familiar with this too. It goes something like this for me: *I already know how you will react if I tell you what I'm feeling and why. To protect my heart, I will keep it inside. You may see it on my face and in my body language, but I can't risk discussing it.*

It is so hard to speak the truth in love, especially in marriage, where the stakes are so high. The risk of rejection is real. It takes courage I often lack. But it is always the right path. It is the task set before us in Ephesians 4:15: "Instead, speaking the truth in love, we will grow to become in every respect the mature body of him who is the head, that is, Christ." Remembering that we are brothers and sisters in Christ brings necessary perspective.

In the season of sitting with a couples counselor, I had already been keeping regular company with a gifted therapist, working on the effects of childhood and young adult trauma. I am so grateful to live in a time of great insight in helping victims of sexual abuse and other situations of deep, deep wounding that linger in the body and brain.

As our life came apart at the seams, I went to see her more often. One day she asked me to think about what I needed, which felt like an entirely new question, especially when my husband was so sick. But it was the right time for me to hear it, part of a larger conversation we'd been having for months. Instead of taking only small measures toward self-care, it was a more profound question about being human and vulnerable, with God-given needs and desires that were legitimate and good. A few days later, I helped my niece take her twin baby boys to the pediatrician's office. When the doctor walked into the examining room, the rightness of the question was confirmed. As one of the boys cried from the discomfort of a wet diaper and my niece changed him, the doctor told her, "He's asking for what he needs, and that's healthy."

Her offhand comment hit home for me—the connection between needs met and good physical and mental health. Needs are complex in adulthood, but the equation is the same. Ignoring them is foolish. It doesn't make us heroic. It turns us into martyrs. It's not good for anyone, especially the people we love.

In the latter half of my fifties, while we were still at the Art House, I longed for a different way to live. It wasn't so much a new longing as an intensifying one. With menopause and its common symptoms of insomnia and low energy levels, I felt age coming on with a stirring inside for life to reflect the changes, but the need to press on in the same intense manner as always ruled the day.

We'd tried to work out better practices for years, but nothing seemed to stick. Amid all that was good and beautiful about our lives, we repeatedly ended up in the same place. We pushed past our limits and lived parallel lives on the same property without really doing life together. When Chuck made plans and commitments that affected us both, and I was the last to know, my heart echoed what I'd once heard a friend say to her husband, "Don't make plans for my life without talking to me!" I grew increasingly resentful and shut down, my words coming to Chuck passive-aggressively, when what I really wanted was to be clear, to be heard.

I did what I could for self-care within a context I couldn't change. Self-care was helpful, as it always is, but ultimately not the thing itself. We needed a sweeping, internal change.

With my therapist's help, I thought hard about the desires and hopes I had pushed down over the years. I searched for words to identify and express them. I wrote everything down in a letter and read it to Chuck in our marriage counselor's office. He received my words beautifully. I needed good rhythms and boundaries to keep us out of physical and relational crises. I wanted to champion him without being demanding *or* having to disappear, and I wanted to be championed for who I am. I needed to discuss what we both wanted our lives to look like moving forward. And I wanted to create a more playful, multidimensional life. I wanted to play a game of Scrabble every now and then, for crying out loud!

There was more to the letter I wrote, but as I revisit it six years later, I can see how much of what we both longed for has come to pass. Much of it through suffering, but also because we had worked hard to name things and understand each other. And the truth remains that we are still in process. We hold both realities together. I'm good with that. Stagnation is standing still; the process is movement.

Becoming a safe place for each other happens little by little. Whether you freeze during conflict and take time to find your words, or you are quick with words, safety comes when you experience being listened to without defense. One experience builds upon another, and trust is created. But, oh, dear reader, what a lifetime of work that is.

If I were sitting at my kitchen table with you today, I'd offer this encouragement: Keep the long view of marriage. If you're in a difficult or seemingly impossible passage, you do not yet know how God will meet you and help you. Of course, there are situations that should not be tolerated. I can't testify to your circumstance. I can only bear witness to what I have seen in our life and the lives of people whose stories we know.

We are all incapable of giving the perfect love and understanding our partner longs for. God helping us, though, we will continue to be changed, able to speak more clearly in love, and hear and receive what we did not have ears to hear earlier. But there is no perfection. And you can't go the distance without accepting that reality. Without accepting imperfection, you will not mature to accept your own failure and the failure of the one you love. Again and again, for days, months, and years, we need to ask Jesus to do what we can't do for ourselves: help us live with kindness and compassion, forgiving each other, just as in Christ God has forgiven us (Ephesians 4:32).

In my Bible, I have a note in the margin next to Ephesians 4:2–3. The passage reads, "Be completely humble and gentle; be patient, bearing with one another in love. Make every effort to keep the unity of the Spirit through the bond of peace." My note says, "For marriage." These words, directed to the church throughout every stage of her history, cannot make sense in a larger context if they don't make sense in our most intimate relationships. But is this a one-and-done effort that can be checked off a list of things to conquer? No, no, no. Never. It is proactive yet entirely dependent, slow, and full of grace. It is the open-palms life of two pilgrim-followers of Jesus choosing each other repeatedly and giving themselves to the mystery and reality of God with us. "Now to him who is able to do immeasurably more than all we ask or imagine, according to his power that is at work within us" (Ephesians 3:20).

I am not a ten-steps-to-anything kind of learner or writer, but there is a way of wisdom that I hold to. *Put yourself and your marriage in the way of good things and wise people.*

At the beginning of our lives in Jesus, we went to a Bible study on marriage. We'd come to faith from an anything-goes social environment, and it was life-giving to begin learning the ways of enduring love and commitment. A little further down the road, we attended a marriage conference, with kind friends sponsoring us for a hotel we couldn't afford at the time. Even later in life, we sat for a day with a bunch of Nashville folks receiving the wisdom of author Dr. Dan Allender, one of the founders of the Seattle School of Theology and Psychology. Over the years, we've talked to trusted friends and asked for prayer, and listened when they needed the same. This kind of conversation bursts the bubble of isolation and frees you from the idea that you're the only couple wrestling with hard things. It is simply not true at any stage of life.

Those are just a few of the opportunities we've had. I encourage you to think of the people and opportunities that you can access. How might you choose to be vulnerable and invest time in the longevity of your relationship? Are there couples a little ahead of you who are inspiring *and* honest about the long road of marriage? Maybe you could buy them coffee every now and then. And how about cultivating friendships with people in similar life stages? This one is so important. We need each other in ordinary times and challenging times. We can't do it alone.

We don't consider asking for help, whether from friends or therapists, a concession or a failure. It's medicine and care. When you have a toothache, you see a dentist. It's not a moral choice. It's simply getting the help you need to function as healthy as possible. It is a priority, and the health of your marriage is no different.

The last thing you want to do is presume you won't need help—that your love and bond are so strong no harm will ever come to you. Instead, count on your metaphorical house being on fire at some point. Plan now for how you're going to cooperatively put out the fire. Never let money be the reason you don't get help. Sell something. Find support for free. Whatever it takes. Keep your heart and mind open and willing to do everything possible to yield to reconciliation and name your own part in whatever fissure and failure you're experiencing.

I'll tell you what I now see as the summary set of questions that have been at the heart of many of our heated discussions and arguments over the years. I think you will recognize them: Do you see me? Do you know me? Does what I do and how I contribute to our lives matter to you? Have you noticed? And do I have your respect?

Oh my goodness, how we need affirmation and recognition from our partner. As you go about your days and nights, speak your admiration and gratitude out loud. This one simple thing, mutual respect and championing one another, is essential. It doesn't come naturally to most of us mere humans, though. It must be learned and practiced, especially in the repetitive life of living in close quarters. Showing respect comes naturally to us when meeting someone for the first time or working with someone, making a new friend. Practicing it daily, weekly, for decades? For some reason, it's not the same. And so it requires a different approach and sensitivity.

One way to do this is to have a check-in. It's a no-threat way of saying, "Let's take a minute and check in with each other." Practically, we find it best to agree to sit for a minute or lie on the bed—essentially, get comfortable. Some of the least beneficial conversations happen simply because we catch our partners in motion and end up standing in the kitchen, each person restless to continue where they were headed.

The check-in includes news of the day, but more importantly: How are you feeling and thinking about the day? Is there anything you need from me? It is information, emotion, and thoughtfulness. We do life with each other in many ways, and transparent conversation should be at the top of the list. The more vulnerable my husband has become over the years, the more there is for me to love. He feels the same.

As I was writing this letter, Chuck told me:

"I remember the idealism of young love, being so attracted and enthralled with you as this marvelous, confounding creature. Then

I began to identify your pain, flaws, or things I disagreed with. I wanted to fix you and tried for years. This was not helpful! Weaving in and out of all that was good in our life we both experienced misunderstanding, hurt feelings, disengagement, judgment, and resentment. Then came a period where we could see things more clearly, at least enough to acknowledge and compromise, confess our failures, and meet in the middle. We'd had enough help along the way to say sincerely, *I see my part in this and ask your forgiveness.* And we did lots of deep soul-work to change bad habits. What makes this the best time yet is that we reciprocate in word and deed, speaking and embodying: *I love you as you are. I accept you and do not reject you. You need not perform for me at all. Not only that, I celebrate you as you are and thank you for all your unique contributions to the life we've made together.* And I still think you are a marvelous, confounding creature."

This is a gift. Especially in this later stage of life, making daily adjustments for mental and physical health. The body has kept the score, and we both require empathy and understanding, sometimes hourly, for chronic-pain issues.

Finally, dear readers, remember all the goodness in your shared story. It is right and beautiful and healing.

In the summer of 2017, the setting with which I began this letter, I often visited my mother-in-law in her memory care home, where she was in the last stages of Lewy body dementia. She could no longer speak coherently. Yet, even as her mind and body were ravaged by disease, her presence was a comfort. I'd sit beside her bed with my hand on her bony hip and feel immediately connected to our history, the people, places, and stories to which Chuck and I belong. She brought me back to our real story, the one so much larger than the challenging moment we were in. Every time I was with her, it was the same.

The people we are connected to help us remember who we are. The more splintered and disintegrated communities and families become, the more the ties that bind people grow fewer, weaker, or absent altogether. Infrastructure is what holds people together. When we do the work of finding our way forward (as often as we need to), we do it for ourselves, for our children, grandchildren and great-grandchildren, nieces and nephews, friends, and their children. Wherever you are, with grace upon grace for second marriages and beyond, remember that one couple's life touches and is touched by so many others.

Chuck and I have celebrated anniversaries in the usual ways, with dinners in restaurants and daylong playdates, but it's been more communal every now and then. I like when this happens. It's a good reminder that marriage is lived in a context, and our lives are joined to others.

When Molly and Sam were little, they invited us to a "somewhat formal" anniversary dinner at our kitchen table in Sacramento. They served spaghetti, brownies, and water. A sweet and perfect meal! Years later, after Molly was married, she and Mark gave us a surprise party for our twenty-fifth. The invitation began: "Come join with us and celebrate the miracle of God's providence and grace." They were young, but they already knew that grace was the main ingredient for marriage. They also knew that the bonds we have with others are what help carry us through.

With our fiftieth anniversary now on the horizon, I know we'll want to celebrate with the people we love, to look at the dear faces of family and friends and say, "Thank you for helping us through and filling our lives with so much treasure."

A few years ago, we went through a lifetime of boxes stored in a large closet. We were seeking a kind of peace and order we'd never had and trying to save our kids from inheriting a mess. It was an overwhelming task that took months, and as with so many things, we're still in process.

We sifted and sorted through archives from our growing-up years and family life. We went through Art House memorabilia, music-career boxes, and correspondence that spanned decades. We read letters from people who'd stayed in our home and emails I'd printed from Molly's first semester in college. Some of our history was hard to revisit, and my heart got weary. But more of it felt like a privilege. I felt rich from all the people we'd known and the stories we'd been part of.

During that same period, Chuck made a short film of our family's life spanning five decades, complete with a fantastic soundtrack. It was a Christmas gift for our children and grandchildren.

A project like this can be so carefully edited, choosing only the happiest photographs and the greatest-hits video footage, that it doesn't present the real story. Chuck found a grace-filled, sensitive way to leave the whole truth in—from glory and shame to fun and folly. There are people we grieve and people who've grieved us, but no one is erased.

There are video clips of beloved relatives who are no longer with us, and pictures of us as teenagers, so lost, yet guided by the sovereign hand of a God we didn't yet know. And then came our own family life. Our small children. Our teenaged children. The full tables of Sunday dinners when they were just leaving home. Graduation parties. Charades at the fireplace after Thanksgiving. Christmas-cookie decorating parties on my birthday in December. The entrance of each grandchild and the special times we've had with them since they arrived on the scene. Our son-in-law, Mark, and daughter-in-law, Ruby, coming into the story at just the right time. None of it translates very well in the telling. But watching something like this is like seeing your life pass before you. It widens the lens and reminds you of all the joy.

Now Chuck and I have a new tradition of watching the film every Christmas season. Each time I watch it, I can't help but think, *We have done so many things wrong, but we've done this one thing right.* We have feasted, we have danced, and we have celebrated the good gifts of God. We've made memories with our children and grandchildren and friends. We've done life-affirming things, and we'll keep doing them, and it's those that we'll never regret.

As we watch the forty-nine-minute film, we cry, we laugh hard, we hold each other and cry some more. The first time Chuck showed me the movie after an all-night editing session, I whispered, "I wouldn't have missed the ride for anything." As with every time I watch the film, this conviction is repeatedly confirmed every day in my marriage (whether the day is one of delight or dry desert).

What we know and trust, as much as God's unconditional love, is that the knot that holds across time requires choosing each other repeatedly. To engage with passion, not simply endure. We were children when we met and fell in love, and naturally we thought like children. Now we are older, but not so old that we are done growing in the knowledge of God and one another, and how to think and act, love and play, as two made one, the life-altering, unfolding mystery of *one flesh*. We know it is the work of our lifetime. I wouldn't miss the ride for anything.

fourteen

THE CATHEDRAL OF GOD'S HANDS

To Parents and Children, Teachers and Students

from Charlie

In the fourth century, Ambrose, the bishop of Milan, was a teacher and musical innovator. He advocated for the then controversial antiphonal chant, and legend has it that when he was just an infant a swarm of bees landed on his baby face and left behind a drop of honey. His dad insisted this was a sign. Sweet elocution would define Ambrose's future.

Ambrose's most famous student was Augustine, the world-weary saint who wrote a series of thirteen books called *Confessions*. In book nine Augustine remembered the music of his teacher this way:

The tears flowed from me when I heard your hymns and canticles, for the sweet singing of your church moved me deeply. The music surged in my ears, truth seeped into my heart, and my feelings of devotion overflowed, so that the tears streamed down.[1]

Giving props to one's teacher has a long history, particularly in the rabbinic tradition. Equally so in the arts. To speak reverently and proudly of our teacher(s) is an act of humility, making clear that the knowledge and skill we possess is not actually all our own. Naming our teachers is good storytelling, revealing significant players in our lives. For example, Dean Estabrook gave me instrumental instruction at Tierra Buena elementary school and then taught me diatonic analysis and harmony (music theory) at Yuba City High School. Not exactly postgraduate study, but no less important to my story. I name Mr. Estabrook whenever I have the opportunity (including naming a song after him on my solo piano recording, *Trout Creek Ranch*).

I have every right to claim I'm a self-taught pianist, but the boast is somewhat inaccurate. I may not have endured years of weekly piano lessons, but my ability to improvise on the piano and arrange music is communally constructed from the history of jazz improvisers and educators and arrangers whose books I studied, including John Mehegan, Dan Haerle, David Baker, Don Sebesky, and Mickey Baker. Directly or indirectly, explicitly or implicitly, the learning gets done. For the autodidact it may be more ad hoc, but no less effective.

My teacher of teachers, my Ambrose, was my dad. All other teachers served the good work he had already begun in me. Like Malcolm Gladwell with his ten thousand hours, my dad believed in the power of repetition. One thousand three hundred thirty-five times he told me: "If you're gonna do it half-assed, then don't do it at all." This stuck with me; glued to my cerebrum. His command applied to a number of things. Especially playing the trumpet, learning music theory, cleaning the garage, and generally avoiding becoming what Dad called "a screw-up"—making me an adult child of an aphorism.

I have so many musical takeaways from Dad, but two are worthy of mention. If you can't play a riff or a piece of music slow with feeling and accuracy, simply speeding it up isn't going to fix it. True that. And when playing in an ensemble, only play just a little bit louder than your neighbor. If you're drowning out those to your left and right, you're playing too damn loud (to use his vernacular). Emotion, accuracy, balance—all currency in the teacher's bank of values and commitments.

I remember Dad's music too, especially his own trumpet tone. I have undiluted memories of sitting in our living room listening to a reel-to-reel tape of Dad singing "Fly Me to the Moon" live at the Table Mountain Tavern in Oroville, California. My own Chet Baker, artist-in-residence.

For a son, a father's influence is everything, and I do mean everything, from blood and bone to sin and glory. One beautiful, positive word from a father can change the course of history. One ugly, negative word can do the same. Then it'll take a hundred beautiful, positive words to shape-shift the unmentionable ache. Only then will dark memories escape gravity. Seek light and space.

At least two great musicians came out of Oroville, California: my father, Bill Ashworth; and Jim Cox, studio keyboardist and member of Dire Straits and Mark Knopfler's band. Jimmy's trio played at our wedding reception, notably held at the odd location of the Yuba-Sutter Fairgrounds. I sat in on trumpet and demonstrated zero facility at playing inebriated. We were all dressed like Bill Evans and Tony Bennett on the cover of the duets record they did—wide polyester shirt collars, bell-bottom trousers, wide ties, and, for me, something called earth shoes. I wore a cream-colored suit purchased at Bluebeards, a contemporary boutique next to the Watt Avenue Tower of Records in Sacramento. Though I didn't know him at the time, it was singer Vince Ebo who sold me the suit. Twelve years later, we'd be in a band together, touring the US and Europe.

Maybe it was protection, or not wanting to fill my already big head any fuller, but my dad felt the need to monitor the throttle on my dreams, keep a governor on what I might think possible. As a young man, he'd had dreams too. Once my sister and I arrived, he had no direction as to how parenting and youthful dreams might be united. Neither did I, but I had clues. The first order of business was to make personal freedom the highest value, followed by a near-wholesale rejection of societal norms. This opened up a whole world of "making it up as you go." I became a jazz improviser and a man committed to improvisation as a value and way of living.

One of the most dramatic examples of this was the home and studio complex that features so much in these letters, called the Art House. It was a twenty-five-years-long improvisation.

———

I have four grandchildren. Bridget, Alfie, Robert, and Brinsley. Each spent hours, days, even weeks at the Art House, our home for a quarter century. Andi created a chest for me and the grandkids—a Papa Art Chest. She packed it with all manner of stuff for making, for arting. Before arting would begin, we'd sing a short, Mr. Rogers–like song. "It's time to art, time to art, it's time for arting!"

Our Art House home was a place where imagination and improvisation were encouraged and boredom repudiated. The whole property was one enormous toy—a kingdom for creativity. Gardens, recording studios, Papa's office with a giant dry-erase board, a field of grass for games, secret nooks in which to hide, bushes for forts, mirror ball for dancing, and, most importantly, Honey's kitchen (Honey is the grandmother name her grandchildren bestowed on her). Each child has been Honey's sous chef and dishwasher.

The Art House was the sort of place where anything could happen. Surprise was built into the walls. Revelation held up the roof. It lived to testify to the power of place in the formation of people.

It was one of those days, a Saturday, when I could smell marinated pork tenderloin from the kitchen. Honey's blend of olive oil, lemon juice, lemon zest, garlic, fresh rosemary and thyme, Dijon mustard, kosher salt, and fresh ground pepper.

Granddaughter Bridget was busy moving from one imaginative game and challenge to another. I was in the big room—the chapel of the hundred-year-old church home we'd created. I was improvising at the grand piano, trying to traverse some hill of inability—start, stop, start, stop. Bridget heard me and came running, chattering, the least taciturn of the grandkids.

Behind the piano was a shelf of keepsakes, including a conductor's baton given to my dad—now mine to keep. It was the showy kind you keep in a case under light. Dad's day-to-day baton was the short, stubby variety. Cork in palm, ice pick protruding. With this short, modest baton he'd conducted musicals, symphonic works, vocal ensembles, marching bands, and jazz bands.

Bridget snatched up Dad's fancy one.

With the glossy baton swinging, she intruded on my improvisation. She wanted me to slow down to a crawl. She was clearly indicating a ritardando. Then she stabbed a staccato punch and rested for two beats—three, four. What's next, I wondered? Straight to accelerando. She was messing with my head. A tyrant with a stick. Or was it a test? A pop quiz? Or simply just play?

A musical conductor controls dynamics and tempo through a language of gestures. Each gesture is a movement of meaning, a sign and signal communicating several musical clues as to the will of the conductor as he or she cares for the music. This includes marking out the time signatures within the composition.

In common time, there are four quarter notes or four basic beats. The simplest form of conducting marks out each of these quarter notes with a gesture of the hand (or hands). A downward movement is beat one. A move to the left is two. Back to the right is three and a smooth bounce up to the one position is four. Embedded in the movement are the tempo (how slow or fast) and dynamics (how soft or loud—communicating intensity, expression, crescendo, decrescendo, and more).

As with everyday life, dramatic, wide, exaggerated gestures mean big and loud. Whereas diminutive gestures mean small and soft— and of course, there are all the nuanced points in between. This is the pleasure of the conductor, offering a different dynamic or tempo to every beat, every note, should the music require it.

While baton and hand movements outline the basics of conducting, interpretive telegraphing is very personal, and usually out of view of the audience. It is private, a familial way of knowing. A lift of the chin and a deep sadness in the eyes, combined with a sweeping movement of the hands, communicates something a mere marking out of time cannot. A skilled conductor uses his or her whole person, body, emotions, and life experience to communicate to the musicians a trustworthy path forward. While highly alert musicians are deftly articulating a complex series of 32nd notes in 5/8 time, their eyes see the conductor inhale and contract neck muscles till red in the face. They know exactly what this portrait of human flesh means. With transcendent performances, music, musicians, and conductor are in sync. Equally venerable. Never passive. Always learning.

Dad conducted in a way that communicated love for his work and people. He had an honorable job to do—help his students acquire facility, learn to care beyond themselves, and have ears to hear.

There is a style of conducting that's never overbearing. The conductor is certainly leading, but more as a goose at the tip of a flying V than an appendage on an otherwise self-sufficient ensemble. To the degree musicians know the sign and signal of this sort of conductor, to that degree they are free. There's no need to stare at the conductor, paralyzed with fear you'll speed up just as the conductor is slowing down.

Relax, be the music, but respect the baton.

The conductor and baton ought to be present somewhere in the musician's field of vision. That way, nuanced gestures of limbs, head, and body woo you to take a brief glance. Every glance and note are a human, communal liturgy. One beating heart with the sound of many.

The creed of the mature, aspirational musician is this: I will follow the conductor, not rigidly but with grace and fluidity, personality and style, doing my part, respecting my neighbor, not clamoring for the spotlight, not taking from the conductor what is rightly his or hers, fully confident that he or she is with us and for us. The conductor is our everyman, empathetic to our challenges, heroic, and truly good.

———

As the twentieth century faded from view, Andi and I were sequestered in a small cabin a few hours from Nashville. We were there for no other reason than our own health and welfare. One afternoon I received a vision in my imagination.

I felt the music surging within me, accelerating. It was allegro with a smile. I could feel the presence of my redbone, musician dad. His copper, kissable forehead came into view. I leaned over him, offered my kiss, and drank in his smell. My eyes vibrated like paradiddles bouncing off the rim of a water glass.

I'd witnessed this scene before—done it, played it. Christmastime, when the children were little and even Dad seemed small and not the least bit threatening. I took his head in my hands and kissed his forehead. One irrepressible act reaching beyond words. The memory of that moment will not leave me.

Now I was with Dad again. Celebrating a different kind of Christmas.

I could tell his heart was well. He'd lost the hesitancy to live and regained the breath of life. He was beautiful. That was all I could think—really beautiful, eager, and full of a frisky hope. He acted like a man who could not wait to show you something he'd discovered or been taught.

What a great feeling that must be, I thought. Nothing feigned, nothing to gain. Every intention, undiluted desire. The pure pleasure of witnessing a recipient take in your good surprise.

Though fleeting, in that moment I realized I am a son, a student, deeply loved. Worn out from striving, all the exhaustion of the universe fell from my shoulders and dissipated. Dad just kept smiling at me as if he knew relief was standing at the door, ready to arrive.

I'd wrestled with identity and worth for so long, always having to prove myself into existence, especially to Dad. Now, out of nothing, came a strange befuddling feeling of something. Peace. I wanted to yell out: "What is this? Can you feel it?"

I heard new music. Simple at first. Andante: single, quarter-note tones played full value by hundreds of instruments in unison, yet none overbearing. Every pitch perfectly in tune. What a gift for my dad. All those years of teaching high school and junior college never hearing music with the rightness he hungered for. *Watch and listen*, he said, touching my hand.

Scene change. Adagio.

We were riverside, both full of imagination and gratitude. This was a wide, open stream, grand yet crossable. With their conifer smells, the monarchs of the forest, tall and regal, stirred old memories of our forest and stream adventures. I could see big-barked Douglas fir, sugar pines, and redwood. Each one providing incense for worship in the cathedral of God's hands.

Wet ferns nudged my leg. I could hear trout singing under the swift movement of the clear, clean water. The trout sounded serious, as if their lives depended on the perfect execution of their trout melodies.

Then came the trout laughter. Trout like giddy schoolchildren.

Rightness was their oxygen. No exhaustive effort expended. They were simply doing what they were made for. Treasured tricky trout. I'd pursued them all my life. Dad had taught me how, and now here he was, pursuing me. Every single thing was alive with rich orchestration, awakening my senses and bringing the deep to where the water lapped the shore.

Love was urging everyone and everything to live for the good of whomever and whatever it bumped up against. I was dizzy from so much excellence.

My dad steadied me. Then he sang "Fly Me to the Moon" as if it was the most natural thing to do at that moment. A minor key among brightness and cobalt light. I let myself cry, just a little. Not too much. I didn't dare fold up and lose my view.

I felt Dad hold me. He would not let me go. That's what I wanted. What I needed. He kissed my forehead. Again and again.

Words passed between us.

I promised you, he said, *if you would take seriously the words of that book* (the Bible), *you would be all right, that you would know and be known. Are you all right? Do you know? Are you known?* he asked.

I wanted to say yes, now that I'm with you. My body wouldn't let me speak. I buried my head in his chest, trembled and groaned. My eyelids, cups of tears.

He held me with his right arm and started to run, quickly. Then he released me and we were running side by side. Like brothers at play we airplaned our arms, zig-zagging to make the wind sing. I could feel the bass gather with power at 20 Hz, the deepest depth of the frequency spectrum.

Eighth-note movements worked the midrange. Staccato sixteenth notes shot through the upper register across the territory of our souls. Stones were under feet, grass against our legs. Clean rhythm. Green nature. Were we even touching the ground? Did we have lift? Ringneck pheasants and coveys of valley quail exploded in flight to our left and right.

No air guitar for us, we played air trumpet. We were twin Harry Jameses in the "Craziest Dream." We were marching-band athletes running sharp angles. I could hear Dad's smoky trumpet tone in my head and he could hear mine. We made no outward sound at all. Nothing. This was music without boundaries, infused by love and rightness. It was nothing short of joy, pressing the valve pistons in rapid unison, my heart singing in ways it had yet to know. This was serious contentment. The sum of imagination and creativity.

We reached a finish line and rested.

Hands on knees, looking up at Dad with a toothy grin, I laughed and shook my head side to side.

The scene changed again.

We sat cross-legged at a small campfire set ablaze on the safety of a huge granite boulder. There was just enough sun left to see a silhouette of the California coastal range and the great Pacific in its pocket. Dad cooked corned beef hash with scrambled eggs and plenty of Louisiana hot sauce. We were eight thousand feet in the air, at least. All I could hear was fire crackle, wind, and my thoughts.

Then I spoke. *Why did you have to die?*

———

Dad was so young and there was so much unfinished business between us. Can you hear the sound of a thousand sighs?

The life trajectory of a son or daughter is no natural arc. More like a maze. Even so, the ideal model of child-and-parent relationship is traditionally plotted as linear. Education begins at birth. Parents teach us the basics. How to communicate. How to walk upright. From our parents, we learn hot and cold, right and wrong, yes and no. It's not all binary and didactic though. A large portion of what we learn is at the tacit level. Year after year, this tacit knowledge takes root in that deep space within us where the words to describe what we know often evade us. Call it epistemological circumvention.

Sometimes, the parent teaches you a vocation. A life's work. This can be a privilege and a problem. In my father I had one parent with two identities, Dad and teacher. It was a privilege to grow up in a home with an educated, working musician. Passing through the living room, I could ask a simple question about counting out a rhythmic figure and be on my way. That is living at the source. Privileged access.

The problem is more difficult to define. I wanted what he had to teach me. Not the way it was taught. I'd watched him instruct and rehearse high school students for years and admired his combination of inspiration and perspiration, seriousness and humor. He was a much-loved and respected educator. I was proud to be his son. Any student who had an issue with Dad was a student who did not want to learn. If you listened and learned, you would become a better musician. Wasn't that the point? Then why did I have a problem with him?

No matter what age I was, or level of maturity, he treated me like a young adult, a gifted, high-potential musician. From this starting point, all of his instruction was problem-solving with excellence as the end result. No time was wasted on positive compliments meant to ease the criticism to come.

Unable to articulate a series of 16th notes in the upper register of the trumpet? Work the problem. Break it down into observable parts—like the components of an engine. Work on your breathing, posture, tone production, and articulation at half speed. Slowing the performance down to a crawl exposes the issues more clearly. Think of instant replay in sports. Watching the play frame by frame, the referee confirms it wasn't a touchdown after all. The receiver's knee was down at the one-yard line before the ball broke the plane.

Watching instant replay, seeing how our brains deceive us, or simply observing how in seven different camera angles one might come to different opinions, is helpful and entertaining. Watching a whole NFL football game this way would be pure torture.

So it is with making music. If the primary interaction between teacher and student is fixing an unending series of problems of performance and musicality in slow motion, it's not difficult to imagine the student eventually feeling like they are the problem. So it was with me. What the teacher meant as time-saving instructive criticism and a bar set high, this son heard as a father's frustration, disappointment, and lack of belief. No cliche says it better than this: "Nothing I did was ever good enough."

Of course no one knew me like Dad. He saw my musical giftedness and the contradictions inherent in my character. Whether he looked at me as a nine-year-old or an eighteen-year-old, he couldn't help but see some part of himself. Which, I imagine, included fears, self-doubt, the challenges he faced and mistakes he'd made as a young musician. He may have said something akin to this only a few times. The amount didn't count. It was in me living at the tacit level—an engine of motivation purring at the sound of silence: "Son, you have no concept of just how hard you have to work to be a successful musician. You have to be the best, put everything into it. If you don't, you haven't got a chance."

It took me decades of producing hundreds of artists to accept the fact that at least 95 percent of humanity learn better when Dad's "work the problem" pedagogy is seamlessly combined with genuine praise, kindness, and respect for the whole person (not simply the musician in need of improvement). Remember Ambrose, the legendary drop of honey, and his lifetime of sweet elocution? In Dad's defense, he practiced this with his high school and college students. Here's my theory why he didn't with me. With a nod to the ubiquitous *Hamilton*, call it the "in the room" assumption.

When I started my artist and producer career, I sincerely thought that great record production was achieved through having fun (enjoying the process and one another), an emphasis on imagination and innovation, ongoing critical analysis of every aspect of the creative process, and laser-focused problem-solving. I still believe this. Though one base assumption skewed the whole thing and I couldn't see it until years later.

My operating assumption about myself, the artists, musicians, and engineers was that by whatever powers put us all together in the studio, we were "in the room where it happens." In *Hamilton*, the characters behind closed doors are history-making politicians. In the "studio where it happens," the music the whole world sings is created. In the grand sum of eight billion people in the world, it is a very small percentage of musicians who create the songs of their generation and beyond.

As Dad had treated me, I treated those in the room as musicians who'd earned the right to be there. I assumed they were confident, highly skilled grown-ups with no interest in gratuitous praise or coddling. With this operating assumption, we would have our imaginative fun and reach for the stars. Unbeknownst to the musicians (until they knew me well), I would simultaneously be in critical-analysis mode, identifying the 73 percent of the music that was excellent and the 27 percent that was not. I would genuinely offer a "great job, guys," but waste no time getting to the business of problem-solving and raising the bar on the other 27 percent. How else would it ever be good enough?

The difference between good and great, better and best is found in the incremental improvement of the smaller percentage. Just as I was taught. Like father, like son.

Later in my career, I learned to mix "sweet elocution" throughout the whole process of recording—making my critique and correction more seamless with the fun and gratitude.

With considerably less drama than with Dad, I was also educated by others—paid instructors at the institutional level teaching me everything from Spanish to concert band and algebra. This is my story, but in general, it is all our story, isn't it? Many teachers, places, and subjects. A diversity of influence whether you name it or not.

While all this learning transpires, our brains and bodies are changing dramatically, progressively preparing us for a life we will make on our own apart from our parents' watchful eyes and helping hands (or those of our teachers). The broad, hopeful goal is that we will run the gauntlet from birth to adult in such a way that we love and respect our parents; make the most of our gifts and talents; become makers, not takers; love our neighbors; and work and play as vibrant, contributing citizens of the planet. No small ask.

Thankfully, many people do make it to this good end. How they get there, though, is never a flat, straight line from birth to roses at the finish. Some children are orphaned, adopted, or born to a single parent. Some of us, through foster care and institutions, have had many parents or guardians.

Some among us are born into challenging circumstances. Not all of us are born healthy or stay healthy as children. Some suffer trauma at a young age, and so the brain develops in uniquely unhealthy ways.

The point being, every person's story is unique, meaningful, and never neutral. No one gets to adulthood without a past.

This same truth applies to our parents, or guardians, and their family of origin and life trajectories (and again, those of our teachers). As with us, their pasts are dense with the data of being human. Consider that some were born into great wealth. Others, poverty. Some fought in wars or suffered famine. They all have their talents, secrets, unarticulated hopes, achievements, gut-wrenching sorrows, pride, and much more. It's out of this complex stew of experience that they parent and teach us.

I suspect that most of us recognize our parents' full humanity too late in the game. They're no longer alive, or their memories and mental acuity are failing. And I'm not talking about "Let me set you straight. I know very well how human they are [or were]." Naming grievances, or what I think was wrong with my parents, is too easy. Plus, I'm already really good at it—no more practice needed. But seeing them as fully human? I missed that chance while they were alive.

I wish I could've known my parents without all the biases I accumulated along the way. I constructed truncated identities for them without ever knowing I was doing it. Then, for the whole of life, I kept them bound to the caricatures I'd created. This doesn't mean that I didn't learn anything of depth about them, or occasionally see them in some new and positive light. Because I did. And I also have the memories of how openhearted, generous, and funny they both could be. They were stellar grandparents too. When we told them we were moving to Nashville, they were unwavering in their support. When it was time to build a recording studio, they advanced us the money (which was nearly their entire savings).

And then, without any warning, Dad was dead, all too young at fifty-nine. Thankfully, my mother lived into her eighties.

When your parents are gone, you can't compare notes anymore, empathize with each other, unravel mysteries, put words to the unspoken thoughts and feelings, show complete transparency, or forgive and be forgiven. You can't champion each other. You can't ask them about their freshman year of high school, whether it embarrassed them that their teeth were so crooked, or why they quit drawing when they were obviously so good at it. The opportunity for such things has passed.

I failed my parents in ways I deeply regret. One incident with the teacher is especially disrespectful. I was enrolled in a jazz ensemble class taught by Dad at Yuba College. At the end of the semester we were required to fill out a teacher performance evaluation. I was critical of the repertoire and the chart-driven approach—I wanted a more improvisational, contemporary direction. I thought the data went straight to HR. I was wrong. Dad read it. He was deeply hurt. Not so much by what I said, but that I would be so insensitive as to jeopardize his livelihood and reputation. This served to confirm afresh to Dad that I was "a smart-ass who thought I knew better" than he did.

So, in the most basic sense, there is a son I wish I'd been—one more faithful, respectful, attentive, kind, and loving. In another, more abstract sense, there is a son I wish I'd been, which was impossible for me to be while they were alive. I was incapable of the necessary insight, curiosity, and empathy to be that son. Nor did I possess the mental health needed. I had to heal significantly before I could see my parents as they really were, and to see myself as I was among them.

Today, as a sixty-seven-year-old man, I'm ready to be the son who asks his parents about everything, who ferrets out every story. I'm prepared to do this and feel no pressing need to illuminate for them what I've thought, felt, believed, valued, and accomplished. My need to honestly know them is far greater than my need to be seen and understood. Maybe this is how you find out you've finally grown up.

It's unfortunate when the parents are no longer alive to receive such maturity and benevolence.

For most of my teens and adulthood, the time I made for my parents was superficial and transactional (which is not uncommon for teenagers). There were seasons when I interacted with them as little as possible. It was a means of survival, a dodge from shame. Always, I was limited in love and curiosity by my own self-absorption, hypervigilance, and patented survival tactic of leaving rooms.

Unfortunately, when I should have been enjoying the last years of my childhood, my focus as a teenager was on premature independence, creating a life I could have authority over, and distancing myself from my parents. Later, at a significant turning point in young adulthood, I got busy being responsible, making a name for myself and becoming a successful musician. Making a name for yourself is a time-sucking, endless task, though. Relationships (parents or otherwise) get wedged into breaks in the action. That's it. They're not the plot.

In the years since my mother passed, I've had the opportunity to process the last vestiges of my parents' lives. Through photos, journals, letters, artwork, report cards, receipts, yearbooks, and more, Mom left us a well-organized history of their own childhoods and marriage. Not too much stuff. Just enough. It's not all new information, but I see it all in a new way.

Now I'm able to see each of my parents as someone's child and grandchild, as young adults struggling to make life work at the most basic level, and as a married couple with bright seasons, dark storms, and their inescapable histories.

The more I understand my parents as people, as I would a friend or neighbor, the more empathetic and forgiving I become toward them. I can see the known or probable source for just about anything I didn't like about them or respect them for. I can see the connections between the pain they endured and the pain they caused.

Several years after my musician father had died, my mother told me, "You know, your dad never had any encouragement from his father regarding music, and so he had no example of how to be with you."

There was a forty-year period when I really could've used this information. That one sentence both wrecked me and made sense of so much of my relationship with Dad. It helped me to see him as a boy who wanted his father to take notice of him, to see what a good musician he was becoming. Dad became the best in high school. He had the encouragement of a teacher, who was a band director, arranger, and former US Army musician. Dad, eighteen years old and fresh from high school graduation, joined the US Air Force to play in the jazz/dance band. Four years later his service ended. Only days before my birth, he came home to Yuba City, formed a band, and got to work playing clubs and dances. Mom had a degree. It was Dad's turn. Funded by the GI Bill, he went to college, earned a music degree, and was immediately hired as the band director at a local high school; he later taught at Yuba College.

Now he had a steady salary plus the extra money coming in from gigs every weekend. Confidently, he went right out and bought a brand-new 1963 Chevrolet Impala. The first thing he did with that car was to load the family up and drive directly to his parents' house. At that moment, showing off a shiny new car his father couldn't afford, Dad was asking without using words: "Do you see me now?"

In contrast to the circumstances I was born to, which were modest, my parents came from far less. It's why they valued so much of what I took for granted and ultimately dismissed as the unnecessary trappings of suburban life. I failed to appreciate how much they'd achieved. It was their labor and grit that allowed me the space to have improbable dreams.

I'd always been a kid who had something in him that needed to come out. I was headed somewhere, out on the horizon, past the predictable, into the freedom and surprise of the unknown. Dad knew how much work it took just to get where he got. Where I wanted to go was beyond his ability to see or imagine.

When I graduated from high school at sixteen (as a junior), Dad pressured me to join the Air Force band. He devised a scheme with a recruiter to arrange an early audition to precede my seventeenth birthday. Once seventeen, my physical and mental aptitudes were tested at a hotel ballroom in Oakland, California (then it would be on to basic training). The night before the exams, surrounded by hundreds of enthusiastic recruits, I used a pay phone to call home. Scared and depressed, I cried and begged Dad to abandon his plan and let me come home. He rebuked and berated me. The message was clear. He'd had it with me. My mother took my side and the fight went offline. I was coming home. I would not be joining the Air Force band.

After the call, communicating this fact to the airman in charge failed. I tried, desperately so, but no amount of explaining penetrated his mission. The next morning I was forced to take all the tests, including a psych evaluation, and a traumatic group prostate exam. In a circle of fifty or so recruits, dressed only in briefs and facing inward, a doctor and enlisted personnel roamed the outer circle. A military voice shouted, "Drop 'em, spread 'em, and bend over." We all complied one by one as the doctor worked the circle, momentarily burying a greasy digit into each of our bums.

The three-hour Greyhound bus ride home gave me time to consider my future. The recruiter would drop me from the band program—this was certain. My girlfriend, Andi, shared my relief. Not only was the intent of the enlistment to "get my head on straight" and later attend college free (courtesy of the GI Bill); it was an obvious ploy to put some distance between Andi and me. We were, it was said, "too serious for our age." In the former, the plan partially succeeded, though not as Dad intended.

My head had never known such pillared clarity. Everything came into focus. I could no longer trust Dad. I was on my own. Time to retire the teacher. His baton could continue marking time, but I'd already left the bandstand. Back home, I fell into Andi's arms, and we took control of our present and future. In a year we'd be married. We were eighteen and nineteen.

And what of the future?

Repeatedly, chronically, I proved to Dad that he was wrong about me. I showed him that my vision of a successful musical life could be accomplished. Then I brought my version of the Chevrolet Impala to his doorstep, over and over, year after year. "Do you see me now, Dad, see me for who I am? Not someone with a music job but an artist living an artistic life?" How foolish of me. How could he not see me? I was the most successful music student of his career. If my father is Ambrose, I am his Augustine.

No habit has been harder to kick than proving my identity and worth—even decades after Dad's death, the impulse remains. It took so long to wind it up, it's taking equally long to unwind.

On November 16, 1971, when I was fifteen, I wrote in my journal: "Most of my day revolves around music in some sort, and it gets to be old after a while, and then it will have some good points too. Sometimes I feel it's time for a day off from band, but I just have to keep pushing. I assume they expect it of me."

By grace, I've been given time and the means to kick the habit of assuming, expecting, and pushing beyond healthy boundaries. It has been my trials and failures (not the successes) that have helped me let go of the son I was, making it possible for me to become the son I wish I'd been and, finally, the son I actually am. One who loves his parents, though always imperfectly. One who respects and gives props to his teacher. One who repents incompletely. And yet, one who receives grace upon grace.

As that graceful son, I release my parents once for all to be fully human, two of God's image-bearers, historical figures with complicated stories, flawed and beautiful, forgiven and admired. I pass no further judgment. Rest in peace until we meet again in the shalom of all that is good, in the cathedral of God's hands.

This seems like such a perfect ending. Cosmically, yes. For this narrative, we're going to need a few closing thoughts.

When the imaginative vision of redeemed father and son came to me years ago, I was grateful. Though I couldn't read it without bursting into an hour-long rain of tears. The first few storms were cathartic. Then I slipped into a classic trauma response of "I don't have time to be ruined right now." So I avoided it. The narrative exposed our mutual failures and my truest desires, and gave artful vision to them repaired and fulfilled, but it wasn't real. I was still living in the in-between of glory and shame, healing and pain. In a world where tears are commonplace. This remains my reality, our reality. Even so, to trust in redemption in the here and now is to believe that nothing remains exactly the same. Changes at the granular level may be difficult to discern, but they are no less real and efficacious.

I believe the vision is a story preceding a trustworthy story to come—a good-will deposit guaranteeing a day when the astonishing rightness of God, people, and place will be present, creatively and cosmically. "'He will wipe every tear from their eyes. There will be no more death' or mourning or crying or pain, for the old order of things has passed away" (Revelation 21:4).

Until that day, there is good life to be lived. Redemption is at work in us and through us. Hope is less deferred than sprinkled throughout our days in just enough measure to believe for a future.

At this point in life, I think my whole family would testify that I thrive as an autodidact improviser and have been amply rewarded for the ability. If you want to paralyze me, place a multifold set of five-point-font instructions in front of me to put together anything. I'm your prisoner. You own me.

When I think back to that winsome exchange with my granddaughter Bridget and the baton, there's something yet to learn. Her conducting intruded on my improvisation. Being her papa, she not only got a pass from me; I delighted in her and every poke of her directorial stick.

When Dad, the teacher and conductor, intruded on my improvisation (during the whole of childhood), my reactions took many shapes, none healthy or happy.

Why the contradiction in responses between Bridget and Dad?

It's no secret that one's most graceful parenting is reserved for grandparenting. It is the blessed do-over with the benefit of experience and wisdom. You've learned to make more of what is of ultimate importance (such as love and mercy) and less of what is less. This explains in part.

As for the child/student and teaching, much has changed since Dad's day, hasn't it? Academics posit there are multiple intelligence modalities, including visual-spatial, bodily-kinesthetic, logical-mathematical, and musical-rhythmic and harmonic. Learning styles are just as plenty: auditory and musical, visual, verbal, physical, social, and solitary are a few. While identifying and naming is helpful, it does not simplify the work of the student and teacher, parent and child, on the whole. It adds to the complexity. Knowing and being known may come with more clues now, but seeing one another clearly and accurately with empathy and compassion is a perennial human problem.

The inability to see one another truthfully is what put Dad and me at odds. The absence of story is what caused it and sustained it.

He had no clue to the longer, deeper story that informed his life, that drove his anger, ambition, and unsatiated need for respect. Since his death, I've been puzzling it together one broken piece of heart at a time.

We see through story. In a way, I have not been able to see my own accurately and helpfully, until I was able to see his. I had to mature beyond isolated memories of the teacher into the fullness of my father's life. It has been decades of work, still incomplete. Still being taught. Still learning.

The last time I saw my father was in Tennessee in the summer of '92, a few months before his death in California. We'd spent the day trout fishing with the whole family. Back home, in the garage putting away the gear, we talked. There in the dim light he saw me: "You are someone who knows what he believes and why he believes it."

Oh, how I wish my own need to be known in that moment had not been so great. I would have returned with a good word, a benediction for Dad, for all parents and children, teachers and students: "So much of how I know what I know has come through knowing you. Lock arms with me, will you? Let's walk and talk. You tell a story first so that my eyes might be open to see more of you."

fifteen

SOIL & SOUL

To the Dreamers, Beautiful and Broken, Wonderful and Weary

from Charlie

Andi and I come from a rural farm community, so *cultivate* is a word I'm very familiar with. In the farm setting, it means plowing or tilling the ground. That is, breaking up the land's surface so natural nutrients and those applied, such as organic fertilizer, can more easily do their work. And, of course, water and sunlight are hugely important. Concerning fruit and nut trees, pruning also plays an essential role.

For example, unpruned fruit trees develop slow-growing and unfruitful shoots. You want your trees to be filled with shorter, fruit-bearing shoots. Pruning also creates space within the tree for sunlight and air. It may seem contradictory, but a tree that grows too much fruit is a serious problem. The branches and shoots cannot support the weight of too much fruit. Branches will snap, and the fruit will fall to the ground and ruin. Worse yet, the tree may split in two, effectively killing the tree and ruining at least some portion of the harvest. I'm proud to say that my great-grandfather Robert Dallas Miller worked as a pruner for many years after migrating from Oklahoma to California. His work contributed to the health and fruitfulness of the orchards around him in Sutter County, California.

From a farming and ranching perspective, this is what I think of and believe about the word *cultivation*. Cultivation is paying close attention to what we make, what we steward, and caring for it, as I've described in these letters. It is intentional, time-consuming, labor-intensive, redemptive, and life-sustaining work. However, understanding and cooperating with the fact that we (the workers) are simultaneously being cultivated are equally critical in the unfolding story of redemption.

In the realm of redemption, or putting all things to right, God is giving his attention to everything he's made and loves—from soil to soul. So while you're breaking up the land's surface to add nutrients, don't be surprised when God breaks up the hardness of your heart and fills you with the nutrients of empathy and mercy or much-needed hope and encouragement. While we create, he faithfully creates in us.

There's a reason Jesus chose these words: "Every branch that does bear fruit he prunes so that it will be even more fruitful" (John 15:2). The pruning metaphor couldn't be more applicable to the human condition. Even when we bear fruit with all our good work, we must inevitably be pruned back. Why? We may bear fruit but be slow-growing. Or, along with our fruitful work, we may grow so big in stature, business, and pride that there's no room left for God or neighbor. Equally perilous is producing an abundant quantity of fruit the world applauds while we die inside or hurt those we love the most. Just like the branch that can't support the weight of the heavy fruit, we snap, and some part of the good fruit falls to the ground and comes to ruin. I know this from experience.

Without God's gracious pruning, all our well-intended, big dreams for contributing to redemption, to the Kingdom come, might amount to very little. We need God's pruning, even when it leaves a scar, a callus, in tree vernacular. Either terminology works. Each reminds us that there's been an intervention. We are not the same. Positively, our fruit may be better in quality than ever, even if it is God's will that it be less in quantity. Accepting God's cultivation of us is another matter altogether. Only time, insights, *aha* moments, repentance, and wisdom sort it out. A gaping, bleeding cut is a tragedy. Five years later, the scar or callus is a story. This is where I was on the road when God met me. Which sounds a whole lot like a Bible story to me.

This letter is a gentle reminder from a fellow dreamer who knows the pain of pruning, bears a few scars and, therefore, stories. From your vantage point, I may be further down the path. If so, you can see me as a scout returning to report on what's ahead. What to look for. What to avoid. And thankfully, I leave you with a witness of the good fruit of God's cultivation of my person.

Dreamers who love and follow Jesus want to do good and serve others, to get right in the middle of the redemption story. Some can take action and self-moderate (counting the cost, as it were). Others, not so much. They are all-in, high-risk improvisers making it up on the spot. Wherever you land on the spectrum, I'm confident of three things:

1. Your intentions to serve and do good, to follow Jesus and love what he loves, are genuine.
2. Your understanding of what is real and trustworthy is still in development. In many ways, you may not know what you don't know. A mix of humility and openness, confidence and grit, and prayerful dependence on the Spirit guide all of this. But on any given day, the mixture can be heavily skewed toward human determination—doing what it takes to make it happen. Sometimes this is courage. Other times, foolishness. You might not know which for years to come.
3. Your expectations for yourself and others, your aspirations for excellence, for the quantity and quality of the fruit of your dreams, may or may not reflect reality. If not, you might be

one of those people who lives in constant disappointment in yourself or others. Confusion, loneliness, anger, and judginess usually appear and wreak havoc.

I've yet to meet a dreamer who didn't think the execution of the dream should be much more straightforward than people are making it. The reality of doing good and serving others is much messier than we could ever imagine or accept. Especially when we are a mess ourselves.

Even so, good dreams come to pass. Redemption occurs. Unique, beautiful changes take place. The soil and the soul are cultivated. How does God do it, and how do we cooperate? I offer my story, beginning with a huge dream initiated by a world-class dreamer.

In 2002, U2's Bono, a dreamer-activist, visited our home to talk about sub-Saharan Africa's HIV emergency (in Botswana, Kenya, Mozambique, South Africa, Uganda, and Zambia). His big dream had redemption written all over it. In short, America is a great and wealthy nation. Many of its citizens are people who profess to follow Jesus. Neighbors around the world are dying, and American Christians can help to play a significant role in saving lives. Were we willing? For the musicians gathered, he asked, Will you join me and others as we use the currency of our celebrity or imprimatur to tell this story till it bears the fruit of love and care? This wasn't just mercy ministry or philanthropy. It was primarily political. The money to help was there. The president of the United States needed the political cover and consensus to act and appropriate it.

It worked. The vast, complicated, likely impossible dream came true. All the storytelling of Bono, Tennessee senator Bill Frist, the church in America, and a ragtag group of Nashville musicians helped to give the most powerful man in the world the political cover to do the righteous thing—care for your neighbor, whether next door or on the other side of the world. As a result, millions on the continent of Africa received lifesaving drugs, most significantly the little ones saved from certain death by becoming infected with HIV through their mother's breast milk.

Admittedly, this was a means and level of participating in redemption I had yet to experience before. It was incomparably complicated, political and divisive, misunderstood, out of control, and imperfect. Yet, on the other hand, it was good, unifying in purpose, and aligned with neighbor love. Thousands of people made small, sometimes indiscernible choices, never knowing whether the collective choices would move the needle. But they did. A strong case for everything that doesn't seem to matter much mattering a lot.

Backstage at a U2 concert in Nashville in 2011, Bono told me, "It all began at your house." Indeed, some of it did. The real story is about how far an imaginative idea can convert to creativity and contribute to the work of redemption in the world. There is no such thing as insignificant good. In Christian terms, this sort of redemptive participation from ideation to action is what Jesus has in mind with the Kingdom coming.

I begin with this dream story because of its massive size. It may have started as Bono's dream, but once he told the story repeatedly, it took on an international life (with an American emphasis on education, politics, and money). It was, in short, a communal story involving thousands of people. It included all the complications that came with big dreams and was monumentally messy. For every story of what went right, you can bet someone was saying, "Yeah, but *what about . . .*?"

Yet we celebrate this big dream and its fruit because good prevailed amid human imperfection and disunity. And I'm confident that many followers of Jesus who were involved were uniquely and surgically pruned that they might go on to bear more and better fruit.

Now let's get personal and granular, shall we?

I've been part of imagining and creating many things meant to positively affect the world—primarily music and the care of people and artists—particularly as a contributor to what has often been called "the intersection of faith and the arts."

The first step in my participation was easy. Music-making was (and is) like breathing and took minimal effort (it was a natural gift that simply needed watering and nurture to flourish). Also, I was predisposed to think that helping people and the planet was part of being human. My parents, grandparents, and great-grandparents frowned upon selfishness and modeled neighbor love through generosity and a helping hand to anyone who needed it.

Participation in shaping our world is a communally constructed activity—not an autonomous solo endeavor—despite all the press the solo fliers get. The truth is, like with the Bono story, no one goes it alone.

Even so, admittedly, participating in community and the stewardship of people remains a problem for me even today (though thankfully less so). I am a dreamer, a boss, a leader, an entrepreneur, and an alpha male. Though a mild-mannered version of the latter. That is, until angered. I do not deny a leadership calling, a gifting to help others, or my ability to dream good dreams. But I start things, then move on. Short-term, high impact, I used to say. (I'm choking at having written the latter. It speaks to the presumption of choice so few actually have.) In the past, I wrongly believed this way of being and doing was psychologically safer. I imagine some readers may be benevolently analyzing and naming me as this or that Enneagram, Myers-Briggs, or Carl Jung classification. I understand. Do your thing.

I need to make something unequivocally clear, though. I have a psychological preference for leading and going on my own to control what goes on. Measuring people, places, and things to effectively lead and work is more than just reasonable due diligence. For me and my broken brain, it is a form of self-protection—undue hypervigilance and self-reliance.

This confession does not undermine or contradict my memories of being a young Christian brimming with new meaning and purpose. In April 1982, I was overwhelmed with gratitude to God and wanted to be in the action of the Kingdom of God coming, present on earth as it is in heaven.

The first steps of participating in redemption were so rewarding—I felt I was helping to make the world better than when I first arrived. I remember small things that were huge in our family life. Especially in contrast to my self-absorbed life before following Jesus. The calling to generosity would be one. For example, the first time we sponsored a child through Compassion, gave an anonymous gift of money to a person in need, or opened our home to a long-term houseguest needing nurture and shelter.

This way of being is at the essence of what it means to follow Jesus, to be an active participant in making known the new way to be human. And generosity was just one spoke on the great wheel of good in the ever-turning business of setting things right. What a life we'd been invited into!

Then came the unexpected ghost of humanity past, broken, bleeding, and honest. I was still a man in need of a savior. And the Savior was ready and willing to prune my proverbial fig tree.

Over time, I discovered I was naturally predisposed to setting only a few things right. Self-protecting and ordering life, I leaned into them with enthusiasm and hyper vigilance. Everything other than what I was naturally good at became a threat to what I was good at! I put my will, affection, and strength into getting those few things right. I prayed and trusted they would be fruitful. Keep in mind, I'm defining *natural* to include gifts and potentialities that had become newly natural through life in Christ.

The rest of my family (Andi, Molly, and Sam) had to buy into my natural *will, affection*, and *gifting* to participate in the sort of potentially redemptive work Art House and my music career had on offer. For the four of us, this included living in an open home with thousands coming through our doors over the years and a few at all manner of day and night. If a family member wasn't called to it at the level I thought faithful, well, too bad—find the strength—this is God's work—let's get to it. Pray as you go. We should be grateful. Ugh.

This was a lot of big talk, hubris, and the product of socialization. Some part of me and my actions were, paradoxically, going in the opposite direction of good. Giving too little credence to other family members' unique giftings, callings, and challenges was, sharply defined, nothing less than spiritual blindness. Again with the paradox. *The dreamer in me could see what was to come, but I failed to see what was.*

As I've said, certain aspects of the music and Art House work were more effortless because of my personality, gifts, and interests. And because I seldom had to clean up my own messes. Without a doubt, I left a trail of them.

It should also be said that gratitude for a reconciled relationship with your Creator does not demand relinquishing your agency to an imbalance of power. Or following a leader who does not listen to or effectually respect your opinion. Time traveling, the contemporary version of me would have been more transparent, inquired of the family and collaborators with consistency and empathy, and listened without immediately developing an assortment of arguments in the bubble outside my head.

For the longest time, I saw the stewardship of people as helping others who were not as blessed as me and my family. This fits in with the "we should be grateful" argument. I believed we were meant to share, be it out of our abundance or what little we might have (à la the widow's mite from Luke 21). Because of my subsistence-farming family background, I think this was more "sharing is caring" than a paternalistic impulse to divide my neighbors into subordinates and dependents needing rescue. Even so, I'm not naïve to paternalism's influence.

My core interests (music, arts, theology) drove me to help and share. This meant participating in artist discovery and development—music and otherwise—and eventually creating a commercial music program at Lipscomb University. Some of the help on offer was music business related and commercial. The balance was teaching, mentoring, counseling, encouraging, and providing clues to probable/intentional paths for people to pursue. Both involved taking action of some kind, furthering people along in helpful ways through influence and resources. I learned from the late sports executive and author Bob

Briner that generosity included sharing any cultural currency I might have accrued. And I did so happily.

But I often did this (sharing and helping) without respecting Andi and the children—the ones I should have cared for first before seeking to help others. I was also naïvely presumptive about *when* to care for others and rarely said no to anything. Saying no to the possibility of doing good? A throttle on my dreams? Oh, I don't know about that.

Apart from my self-protection strategies, I lived a boundaryless life and dragged Andi and the kids along with me. I knew I could say no. I did not have to work for God's love. Grace through Jesus was not simply sufficient but, in fact, everything. The problem was I did not want to say no. I liked how it made my brain feel, even when yes upon yes added up and my body demanded a week in bed or else. Sadly, there was also a younger me dwelling within who believed saying yes was expected of him (in this sense, a part of me felt I had no agency in the matter).

Let me pause my confession for a moment to look at the positive. Analysis without grace and gratitude is too easily reduced to data. We are not human calculators but whole people, complicated, broken, and beautiful.

I have truly enjoyed playing a large or small role in seeing all sorts of people advance in their unique callings. I liked identifying those people I thought had potential—again, usually about music, but also about any skill and ability with transferable potentialities. ("Since you are a self-professed introvert, your deep love of music and obvious administrative gifts might be a good fit for music publishing.") Fred Smith, the founder of the Gathering, blessed me one day, affirming this role. He wrote a short essay and sent it to me, along with a note that said, "This is how I think of you." The essay examined "the principles for organizing extremely talented and sometimes difficult and idiosyncratic people." Perhaps I am the "one person who acts as 'maestro,' or the 'practical dreamer,' organizing the genius of others."[1]

This ability to organize the present and imagine the future with ease and accuracy was, I believe, a spiritual gift (as in 1 Corinthians 12:1–11).

I take no credit and watch in grateful amazement at all the cosmic betterment these people have been up to over the decades—especially my adult children. Good dreams have come true and borne fruit.

But after thirty-plus years believing I'd been working in service of others, I had an epiphany of overdue self-awareness. I was far better at a hybrid of service and transactional relationships than serving others in the purest sense. Not that I was overtly selfish or just out for myself. I hope I haven't been. But I'd created a way of serving others that fit neatly with my dream-making—a burning need to accomplish as many good things as possible, as quickly as possible. Didn't everyone want to efficiently achieve the maximum amount of good, 24/7?

Yes, in theory, most people do. But *accomplishment* and *efficiency* are not words we associate with everyday, often messy, and on-no-timetable human relationships.

For example, picture me in the recording studio visiting with a young artist, enjoying his company and giving him life counsel and career advice. The visitor would usually express gratitude for the help but know the visit would be short and not presume this interaction would continue. ("Thank you for meeting with me. I know you are incredibly busy.") Naturally, this presumed boundary worked for me, and I favored it. Good meeting. Back to work I went.

I was baffled by the people who wanted more than these helpful one-and-done interactions (which I later understood to be just about everyone, except people similar to me). Gifted, good-hearted people wanted to spend substantive time with me as a person, have unscheduled conversations with no predetermined end, and be in my orbit (and vice versa) whether we worked together or not. They wanted more than a transaction of information, expertise, and "eyes to see" intuition. They wanted what most people still want and need: human interaction and nontransactional relationships. It took me years before I understood that this alone is the good dream of many.

This is what Andi had been asking of me our whole lives. Personally, as a husband, yes. But communally too.

In retrospect, I failed miserably at the work of deep personal caring. Especially so with anyone who might be the slightest bit needy, demanding, illogical, or simply lonely. These normal humans scared me. I excluded them from my calling, keeping the easy humans close. Andi had done all the unselfish personal caring. I'd done something, but it wasn't that. The exception was I did experience a deeper level of friendship and mutual care with a small group of men and a few artists. Thankfully.

My participation in the redemption of all things had accomplished much in volume. I have to be honest about this. It's just addition. More hours worked plus more projects and interactions equal more potential for good and redemptive outcomes. I have to be equally transparent about the cost of this volume of work to those I love and the cost to my own mental and physical health. As mentioned earlier (in "Dangling over the Cliff and Other Dangers"), Andi and I use the phrase *too-muchness*. It describes a tipping point when all the productive work, my imaginings and creativity, and artist/people development overwhelmed our well-being and became too much. Too-muchness proved to me that even good dreams can do damage.

The imagination is a way of knowing oneself and the world. Its fruit, creativity, is how we make the world we want to live in. For some of us, repetitive use of the imagination is not only the way we make sense of the world but also how we keep moving and stay alive. If we are not imagining what's next and creating it, we lose our sense of self-worth, our reason for being. The problem and the glory of the imagination is that a single use of it is so powerful as to create enough work for thousands of people over a lifetime. The imagination knows no neutrality. Even if creativity never appears, it still has effects and consequences on the one imagining. Even those closest to you can feel the impact of your imagination on their minds and bodies. It is that powerful.

During our years of too-muchness, Andi had her own unique calling to writing, speaking, and caring for people and place. A full-time job that was needed and appreciated. Imagine having your significant, meaningful labor constantly added to with more work you did not imagine, choose, or agree to.

How did this come to be? Doing good and hurting the one I love the most?

So much of my social formation was influenced by the migrant and pioneer spirit of the West (enduring any hardship to arrive somewhere new to achieve something new), artistic individualism, and paternalism. The latter is an enmeshed way of thinking and being in American history and its citizens, especially among men racially divided as white. Fueled by an imbalance of power and resources, *paternalism* is the sociological driver behind the worst of the American experiment—one among a very long list. However, enslavement, land theft, and the subjugation of women and people of color would undoubtedly be at the top.

A standard, more nuanced characteristic of paternalism manifests itself as taking responsibility for people, places, and things that are not one's responsibility. When people are the focus, paternalism's impulse may be to oversee/help those who do not seek or need oversight and help. People may vehemently reject it. This can be baffling to the paternalistic mind.

Artistic individualism blends the free and unfettered imagination of the artist with individualism (chronic and stubborn independence and autonomy).

The ethos of the American westward migrant, or immigrant pioneer, is resilience, never taking no as the final word, and surviving against all odds.

I've been too slow in grasping the enormous influence these three have had on me as a man, son, husband, father, artist, and citizen. Winnowing paternalism and toxic individualism out of my life is fulltime work. I want to do the work, though. My vision for life improves as the old lenses slip and fall away. What I see inspires and gives new and better direction for my callings. In short, I am grateful that God loves me enough to prune me with precision and gentleness. He has never ceased cultivating me, redeeming me.

I've learned that *people stewardship* in the church is always about followers of Christ caring for each other side by side, before it is ever about following a leader, regardless of the big dream or perceived good they may have on offer (e.g., influence, knowledge, and resources). Authentic people-care is mutual stewardship, inclusive and broader than it is tall. It accounts for exemplary leadership and imaginative dreamers, inviting diverse voices into every corner of life, listening as much as talking and observing as much as doing.

Didn't I know this before? Yes, I knew it. Knowledge is not wisdom or embodiment, though. Taking my own medicine as a songwriter: "Truth to be understood must be lived. You can only possess what you experience."[2] Nuggets inspired by A. W. Tozer, if I remember correctly.

I've seen mutual stewardship in the Anglican fellowship my daughter, Molly, and son-in-law, Mark, call home. Expertise, resources, and influence are not the sole domain of the charismatic leader with an imbalance of power on their side. Good can do its thing in the church and world without a paternalistic, top-down transactional approach.

Is there still a spiritual calling to leadership, counsel, and teaching? Is there expertise to be shared? Gifts to give and receive? Does the world still need its dreamers? Yes, and double yes. How this manifests in our relationship with one another and the world is always a work in progress. It is good seeking to do better. The work of a lifetime. Imperfection and faithfulness are not at extreme odds. They've had plenty of time to develop ways of working together, of participating in the redemption of everyone, everywhere, and in everything.

INCREMENTALLY CHANGED INTO THE IMAGE OF JESUS

My friend Steve Garber, a gentleman and scholar, uses the word *proximate* well. As you might imagine, it means something like "not quite there," "almost," or "still a ways to go." I have made my "peace with the proximate."[3] I have failed miserably right in the middle of the field of plentiful harvest, not once but too often. Until the remaking of all that God loves is complete, our participation in the story of redemption is proximate. Though tinged with sin, any good we are privileged to participate in is a promise from God fulfilled and something for which to be grateful.

For most of my theological life, I've used a phrase adapted from something Os Guinness explored in depth in his book *The Call*. Our calling is to be Jesus-centric, creative people everywhere and in everything.[4] I believe this with *every* part of my person, and hope I have embodied it.

The Kingdom work of setting everything right is communally constructed by all of us, conducted by the hand of God at work within the Membership (to borrow from Wendell Berry). I have always believed this too. Now I've lived it. I have possessed this truth. By grace, it is in my grasp.

All of us are in the business of carrying out Jesus' plan for people, place, and things—*his will* for redemption and how we participate. Costly lessons to learn for this solo entrepreneur and family.

I want to add a word about the stewardship of time. I have felt there is never enough time to do things right. I have lived with the anxiety that everything other than my work is a threat to my work. I have thought myself the ultimate multitasker, achieving much because of my perceived ability to (mixing clichés) keep more balls in the air while playing three-dimensional chess.

Busy entrepreneurial people (even in doing great good) purpose to or unconsciously create the impression that they are multitasking and doing much. In truth, they are very often getting more done than others. But each thing they get done is an abbreviation or approximation—it is the tip of the spear with little to no shaft. (In my case, the most apparent abbreviation and approximation have been relationships.) You can appear full of energy and vision, even change the world, when it is God who is full of energy and vision to change you, just as he promised.

Participation in the redemption of all things is all about Jesus, all about the Lord calling, equipping, and ultimately forgiving, giving ever more grace as the wheat where we have farmed gets separated from the chaff, and the good fruit is culled from the spoiled.

So we pray to have learned—to be wiser today than yesterday. We grow and are ever changed—this is what the Kingdom coming is about, and what it means to be incrementally changed into the image of Jesus—and we find again and again that Jesus cares about what we do and how we do it. He does call us to particular work (even work that is more visible than others)—but his love is never contingent on what we do, who we are, or what we can pass on to others.

I was tagged on Instagram a few years back and clicked through to see why. The photo was the underside of a forearm. Filling the whole fleshy space was a tattoo that read "It's not just about creativity. It's about the person you're becoming while you're creating." Yes, I said that or wrote it. Which and when are lost to time. Someone found it, though, and put it on their body.

I close with this tattoo to reemphasize, once again, that this work of dreaming good dreams of loving redemption and care has two parallel tracks. First, people, places, things, and all the creative work accompanying them. And then there is you.

God, in his mercy and grace, is cultivating you. Revisit those verses in the Bible about pruning—often, as needed. It's all there. Here's Jesus: "I am the true vine, and my Father is the gardener. He cuts off every branch in me that bears no fruit, while every branch that does bear fruit he prunes so that it will be even more fruitful" (John 15:1–2).

Be just as eager to grow and change for good as you are to faithfully cultivate your patch of the earthly garden. How all this plays out in the hidden details is the purview of the Spirit of God. Listen and watch. Cooperate by doing, of course. But also by not doing. Instead, just be. Allow yourself to sit right in the mystery of it all and not have it all figured out or need to; accept the proximate nature of all your efforts; and love God and those closest to you with the love that will not let you or anything of value go. This is the dream.

sixteen

HOPE FROM FURTHER DOWN THE ROAD

To the Beloved

From Andi

I wonder if you carry an invisible knapsack of words like I do. These words help me make sense of things, deepen my understanding, guide my path, and give me hope. We eagerly pick them up, and they become essential to our vocabulary. For me, they are words like *vocation*, *faithfulness*, and *dependence*. And *fruitful*. It's been years since I tucked this last one into my bag.

One hot summer weekend in July 1993, I left my children with a friend and took a road trip to Asbury Seminary in Kentucky for a L'Abri conference. Traveling somewhere alone in the years when Chuck toured so heavily was unusual. Someone had to care for the home and hearts in Nashville, and we didn't have family in town. But this time I was determined. And excited. I loved the L'Abri community, and this gathering was close enough for an easy drive. I packed some clothes and a toothbrush, *The Brothers Karamazov* for nighttime reading, and a journal with lots of empty pages for taking notes. All the essentials. With four hours on the open road, sunny skies, a bag of snacks, and a book on tape, Mama was having fun!

I found a few friends at the venue, and we sat together with our open notebooks. There were people of all ages, from college kids to grandmas and grandpas. Everyone came hungry to learn from teachers who believed Christianity speaks to all of life. I was eager to hear from Dick and Mardi Keyes, and professor Jerram Barrs, the gentle English scholar and gardener—all people I deeply respect.

But in the end, Wim Rietkerk from Holland L'Abri gave the words I took home with me and thought about for years to come. His talk, titled "The Search for Success," in its essence was about seeing life through the Jesus lens of fruitfulness rather than cultural ideas of success.

Over the following decades, whenever the word *success* was used in an unhelpful way, I had an internal reaction. I questioned whether it fit me, my family, friends, and the narrative of our lives. The meaning was always too narrow. It failed to consider a broad and realistic range of people and circumstances.

There is legitimate joy and satisfaction and gratitude for the many kinds of successes we might experience as people. Just think of all the things we celebrate—graduations, beautiful artwork, high school football games. Win or lose, if one of the football players is someone we love, we are the loudest people in the stands. We cheer them on because we delight in them.

Many of our successes are quiet and hidden. If you just made it through the week with a newborn who doesn't sleep, that, my friend, is cause for celebration.

But when the word *success* asks us to measure the value of our life by metrics, the meaning becomes not only troubling but, in a sense, meaningless.

Maybe you've experienced something like this scenario where a well-meaning friend used the word *success* in a conversation.

Questioning friend: "I see that you're doing interior design now. It's definitely your gift. You're so good at it. Are you having any success? What's your social media presence like?"

With the reality of capitalism assumed, the emphasis of success and platform can send dehumanizing questions pinging through our minds and knotting our stomachs: *Have I done enough, achieved enough, or sold enough? Do I have sufficient notoriety, money, and influence?*

This definition of success concerns numbers, quantity, and ubiquity. How will we ever know when our numbers are high enough, though? On our own, we likely won't. Don't worry. There's a gatekeeper somewhere waiting to inform us. But if we live by their definitions of success, we live by their rules. The hope I bring from further down the road is that we don't have to. Not really.

Years ago, Chuck returned home from one of his many music business trips to New York City. I asked him to fill me in. He was scheduled to meet with the legendary Clive Davis or a senior executive below him. While Chuck was sitting in the record label lobby, an assistant came out to speak with him. The assistant wanted to know where Chuck's productions were currently charting on the Billboard 200 albums chart. Taken aback, he frustratingly answered, "There's two, at number thirty-three and number sixty-five." The young man informed Chuck that he'd have to meet with the senior exec. Clive was only taking meetings with producers currently in the Top 10.

My husband has been to number one. He's a musician and loves charting as much as the next artist, songwriter, or producer. But his number one priority is creating *good*. He knows there's no more fickle creative relationship than one that favors chart action over imagination.

At its worst, this chart-like way of naming human value leaves out whole swaths of people the world over whose callings and circumstances don't fit the metrics or categories. And when the measurement system applies at all, it is fleeting, a roller coaster of ups and downs. One day you're in; the next, you're out.

Perhaps you've felt this sting too? You may have received some exciting awards and recognitions for your work one year and struggled to make ends meet in the following years. Or, like many, you've experienced an illness that's left you severely limited. You might be a student (or the parent of one) whose grades fluctuate. If so, report-card time can be misery or merriment. These examples, and hundreds like them, can cause a momentary or extended identity crisis.

Who are we if no one pays attention to us? Who are we if opportunities or grades take a dip? If we can't do all we once could because of health or age? Are we still people of value? Is success only for the strong, for those who have no struggle? Is success only for a specific age group and not for children or the very old? Is success only for the powerful and wealthy, the dominant caste?

A million times no.

It's because the word *success* can be so wrongly used and interpreted that I've replaced it with *fruitfulness*. It's at the top of my knapsack of words. I don't have to dig for it.

I think of several families I know personally who quietly and humbly serve Jesus with their high wealth and influence. I certainly don't know the details because they would never talk about it. But I know they follow Jesus in humility and serve the greater good with what they've been given.

There are others whose wealth and influence are cruel, self-serving, and corrupt (history is filled with stories right up to our current time). They might be considered successful on someone's measurement scale, but they are not fruitful.

Unlike the culture's use and definition of success, a Jesus-centric definition of fruitfulness always begins with *faithfulness to a loving and caring life*. It is quality and quantity, but always quality first—as in the standard of being human into which Jesus invited his followers. And as for quantity, in the realm of fruitfulness, one might be plenty and a million too many.

We can see fruitfulness in others but are wise not to tally it for ourselves. Though we participate in God's loving work in a million different ways, as with the gift of grace, there's no room for boasting. The creation of a fruitful life is God's work. It flows from the love of Jesus and our union with him. If we boast, we boast of his love and care.

Here's the beautiful, remarkable thing about turning toward fruitfulness and away from success. Fruitfulness isn't bound to the moment we're in or only what's visible and measurable. The work of God's Spirit can't be contained, quantified, categorized, bottled, labeled, or counted in trophies. There will be fruit when some measure of love, joy, peace, patience, kindness, goodness, faithfulness, gentleness, and self-control grows inside us and moves into the world through us (Galatians 5:22–23). We can count on fruit if we remain in his love (John 15:1–17).

Day by day, God is calling us to things that might have the quality of eternal worth. But we don't have to know how it will all shake out. I hope this is encouraging and freeing. Use your freedom to serve one another in love. Rest in a deep sense of dependence on Jesus to make lasting fruit. It's what he does. Plus, remarkably, he's invited you to become a worker in his proverbial fruit-bearing vineyard. If you've accepted the invitation, if you remain in him as he remains in you, you're doing it.

It's impossible to know all the unseen work that God is accomplishing in our lives, in our time, in the life of the world.

This is a truth to stand on, dear ones. Let it settle your weary hearts. Your hope is not deferred. It is happening now.

Some years ago, when I was still technically in middle age, I came across this passage at the end of Psalm 92: "They will still bear fruit in old age, they will stay fresh and green" (v. 14).

I'd been searching for a way to think about aging that wasn't silly or negative. I looked for older people, women especially, who were comfortable in their own skin and yielding to the years with grace and an open heart. They were a breath of fresh air when they crossed my path as friends, through books or in my travels. Inspiring.

The words in Psalm 92 hit me like that, only much deeper. They grounded me in a better reality and directed my trust to the right place. Bearing fruit, staying fresh and green—those words had life in them, the life of Christ. Wrinkles, declining energy, loss of all kinds, illness, or gray hair—none of it seems to hinder God's ability to make his people flourish like a palm tree and grow like a cedar of Lebanon (v. 12).

Since the day that passage stood out so clearly, I've made it my prayer. As this book ends, Chuck and I are standing together, hand in hand, praying for ourselves and you, dear readers, following the way of love in a world of hurt. Join us as we pray together:

Be with us, O Lord, as we raise our children, love our families, face a diagnosis, and seek the peace of our city. Though our lives are small and the challenge is great, help us to know, individually, what it looks like to care for the poor and the needy, the refugee, the oppressed, the imprisoned, the hungry, and the lonely. Open our eyes and ears to injustice, more today than yesterday, more tomorrow than today. Stir our imaginations and bless our creativity—the work of our hands and hearts.

Help us be faithful by your grace to the stories, callings, and stages we're in, and to put our trust in Jesus alone. Guard our thoughts and ambitions against the fleeting satisfaction of counting and measuring. Reveal to us, and then through us, your economy of beauty and goodness. Let it be said of us that we are your people.

Water us, O Holy Spirit of God, that we may stay fresh and green, bearing fruit all our days. May your unfailing love be in us, with us, and for us, as we put all our cares, concerns, hopes, and dreams in you. For we know from experience that great is your faithfulness, and you alone are worthy of all honor, praise, and glory, amen.

ACKNOWLEDGMENTS

Credit to Erin Healy and Elisa Stanford for editing and wise counsel on our early drafts. To Don Pape of Pape Commons, our agent and advocate for twenty-plus years, thank you for finding the perfect home for this book. Lisa-Jo Baker (editor) and Damon Reiss (publisher) of HarperCollins's W imprint, you understood it from the jump and added a substantive vision for what the book could become. Lisa-Jo, kudos for bringing such heart, encouragement, and skill to the editing. You have our trust and gratitude. Big thanks to the whole W team—editorial, marketing, and PR.

Without the following people playing myriad roles (including family, messenger, wise one, facilitator, friend, and collaborator), this book's stories and meaning never would have happened. Profound gratitude to Jimmy & Michelle Abegg, Dane & Maggie Anthony, Brown & Debbie Bannister, Nick & Krista Barré, Jerram Barrs, Diana Beach Batarseh, Margaret Becker, Kenny & Laura Benge, Wendell Berry, Richie Biggs, Bono, Doug & Terri Bornick, Brent & Mary Ann Bourgeois, Virginia Bousquet, Ashley Boyd, Bob Briner, Ned & Leslie Bustard, Michael & Julie Butera, Chris & Alice Canlis, Nancy Carroll, Jeff Coffin, John & Laura Cowan, Craig & Judi Daniels, David & Sarah Dark, Guy & Marissa Delcambre, Scott & Christine

Denté, Joanne Devine, Mark DiCicco, Ciel Eckard-Lee, Mark & Jan Foreman, Fence Jumpers Book Group, Mike Fernandez, Mako Fujimura, Steven & Meg Garber, Allison Gaskins, Liz Goodgame, Jessica Graeve, Amy Grant, Jenny Green, Troy & Sara Groves, Os Guinness, Denis & Margie Haack, Kate Harris, J. C. & Barbara Haynes, Darrell Harris, Bill Hearn, Billy Ray Hearn, Allan Heinberg, Steve Holsapple, Andrea Howat, Penny Hunter, Gina Hurry, Katy Hutson, Richard Kapuga, Dick & Mardi Keyes, David Kiersznowski, Demi Kiersznowski, John & Jean Kingston, Donna King, Nancy King, Katy Krippaehne, Joan Kudin, Lynne Lyle, Sandra McCracken, Bruce McCurdy, Douglas & Lisé McKelvey, Jenae Medford & Chris Rose, Pat Minor, Byron Borger, Don Murdock, Louis & Mary Neely, Leah Payne, Eugene & Jan Peterson, Steven & Amy Purcell, Russ Ramsey, Brad & Holly Reeves, Sally Reid, Carly Ripp, Mark & Leanne Rodgers, Michael Roe, Edith & Francis Schaeffer, Steve Scott, Jenni Simmons, Aaron Smith, Bob & Kathi Smith, Fred Smith, J. D. & Cleo Smith, Roger Smith, Scotty & Darlene Smith, Edie Spain, Viola Weinberg Spencer, Jennifer Strange, Jay & Jamie Swartzendruber, James Sweeting, Switchfoot, Nate & Cassie Tasker, David & Phaedra Taylor, Steve & Deb Taylor, Jim & Kim Thomas, Steve Turner, Jan Volz, Judy Weber, Dallas Willard, Boomer & Paula Williams, Joy Williams, Shane & Stacye Wilson, Peter & Michelle York, and Clark & Karoly Zaft.

A special acknowledgment to three people groups: First, to all the artists who created on the Nashville Art House property, recording and otherwise. Thank you for gracing us with your presence and talent. Second, recognition and gratitude to the houseguests and those who dropped by or attended retreats, celebrations, concerts, conferences, and weekly events. You brought the Art House to life. Finally, applause and fireworks for all the Art House volunteers—from the first brush of new paint to the twentieth-anniversary celebration and beyond. You did it.

To our California and Tennessee families, thank you for the fun, love, and support. Mark & Molly Nicholas and Sam & Ruby Ashworth (the big kids), gratitude for your relentless pursuit and care of us. Being your parents and in-laws is pure joy and poetry. You inspire us to no end. Grandchildren: Bridget, Alfie, Robert, and Brinsley, when you read this book (and of course you will, someday), we hope you see how much you've been loved and cherished. Each one of you is a bright star.

RESOURCES

ART HOUSE COMMUNITIES

Founded in 1991 by Andi Ashworth and Charlie Peacock (Ashworth), the Art House in Nashville, Tennessee, quickly emerged as a unique artistic hub for rich hospitality, conversations of consequence, and imaginative creativity. For twenty-four years, a one-hundred-year-old renovated country church was their home and the primary setting for their work as founders and executive directors of what became Art House America, a 501(c)(3) nonprofit. Since 2010, the work has grown to include additional Art House locations in Dallas, Texas, and Saint Paul, Minnesota (as well as a sister organization in Birmingham, Alabama—InSpero), carrying on the Ashworths' original vision of promoting creativity for global flourishing and nurturing individuals eager to explore an artful, faithful life.

Art House founding workers include artist manager and record executive Nick Barré; writers Douglas McKelvey (*Every Moment Holy*), David Dark (*Life's Too Short to Pretend You're Not Religious*), and Russ Ramsey (*Rembrandt Is in the Wind*); and the late Jay Swartzendruber, writer for the Billy Graham Evangelistic Association, editor of *CCM* magazine, and publicist for Charlie's re:think and Steve Taylor's Squint record labels.

Writing has always been at the heart of the Art House ethos. It is providential that one of the first monetary gifts given to the work of Art House was a hundred-dollar check from the much revered writer Frederick Buechner. Between 2010 and 2018, Andi, as editor-in-chief, and Jenni Simmons, as editor, curated the *Art House America* literary blog, archived and available for readers at arthouseamerica.com.

For more information on the individual Art House sites and missions, please visit the following resources.

Art House Dallas, Dallas, Texas, USA

https://www.arthousedallas.com/

Principal leadership: Founder Brad Reeves, chairman of the board for Art House Dallas (AHD). Along with his wife, Holly, Brad is an active philanthropist serving the needs of Dallas and beyond. Marissa Delcambre serves as the executive director for AHD. Marissa's husband, Guy Martin Delcambre, is a storyteller, poet, and pastor and serves as director of formation and sustainability. AHD has an adventuresome and prolific history of events and ongoing programming, including the Origin formation series, which seeks to establish a wholeness and connectedness between spiritual formation, imagination, and the arts; the Deploy program, where AHD connects local artists with underserved communities; Art House Exchange, a pub gathering that exists for the exchange of ideas and creative discussion across artistic mediums; and monthly Awaken Creativity groups, which create consistent community for participants.

Art House North, Saint Paul, Minnesota, USA

https://arthousenorth.com

Principal leadership: Founders Troy and Sara Groves. The Art House in Nashville had long been a place of nurture to the Groveses. It was a dream to provide a similar space in the Twin Cities. In 2011, the dream caught fire after Sara and Troy visited a one-hundred-year-old church building for sale in Saint Paul. Shortly thereafter, they purchased the property for Art House North, moved their family into the city, and opened their doors to enthusiastic community support. Art House North is known for imaginative, diverse events, including concerts, theater, square dances, artist responses to social issues of immigration and creation care, and their popular yearly songwriters' workshop.

Art House Nashville, Nashville, Tennessee, USA

https://www.arthousenashville.com/

Principal leadership: Nathan and Cassie Tasker. The Taskers were appointed codirectors for Art House Nashville in 2016, moving with their three children to the original Art House site in Bellevue, Tennessee, to continue the work of hospitality and teaching begun by Andi and Charlie. After a busy tenure of concerts, speakers, vocational counsel, and operating the recording studio between 2016 and 2022, the original Art House property was sold and Art House Nashville pivoted to a virtual and pop-up model. Nate and Cassie are dual citizens, spending Tennessee winters in the summer of their native Australia. In addition to their Art House work, Nate continues as a much-loved speaker and musical artist for Compassion International (nathantasker.com).

InSpero, Birmingham, Alabama, USA

https://www.inspero.org/

Principal leadership: Founder and CEO Gina Hurry. InSpero is very much a sister organization to Art House, in ethos and friendship. Andi and longtime Art House contributor Steven Garber are board members. Birmingham-centric, InSpero seeks the peace and prosperity of the city through gatherings of beauty, grace, and radical hospitality—cultivating hope and meaning for all people of Birmingham by caring for creatives and organizing opportunities for them to share their beautiful gifts with the city. The mission is clarified further by this important statement: "As InSpero acknowledges the deep racial wounds of our city, our posture is one of kneeling, not standing. We grieve the injustices suffered by people of color through systemic oppression. We desire to listen, learn, lament, and be part of the healing of our city. We kneel in prayer and repentance and stand with those who recognize and work for racial reconciliation and equality."

Essential words that also reflect the Art House posture and mission of Nashville, Saint Paul, and Dallas for their cities, and beyond to the whole world.

RELATED COMMUNITIES

In 2007, Charlie cofounded Wedgwood Circle with a group of friends composed of investors, philanthropists, and artists—led by the industrious Mark Rodgers, who arranged for Bono to meet with Nashville musicians at Andi and Charlie's home in 2002. For fifteen-plus years, Wedgwood has stayed true to its goal of promoting the creation of good, true, and beautiful entertainment, including film, music, literature, fashion, and much more. Other cofounders include: David Kiersznowski (also a partner with Charlie in Twenty Ten Music and the development of recording artists the Civil Wars, Ruby Amanfu, and the Lone Bellow), artist/educator Makoto Fujimura, and "Wedgwood facilitator of meaning" Steven Garber (the latter two also listed in the following pages). Andi and Charlie count Steve and Meg Garber among their most beloved peers and friends. Mako and Charlie have been friends and mutual advocates since the advent of Art House and Mako's International Arts Movement. In addition to cofounding Wedgwood, Mako, Andi, and Charlie worked with John and Jean Kingston to create OQ Farm in Woodstock, Vermont (along with painter Bruce Herman, former CIVA executive director Cam Anderson, and Tim Dalrymple, president and CEO of *Christianity Today*, among several others).

In 2015, Charlie founded the Commercial Music program at Lipscomb University in Nashville, Tennessee, designed to reflect the ideas and practices that have led to his own sustainable music career for fifty-plus years. After serving as director of the program, as well as director of the School of Music, he passed the baton to a former mentor, decorated music producer Brown Bannister. For students and parents looking for a program of this kind, see more information in the coming pages.

Charlie and Andi also support the good work of these related, affinity communities: the Rabbit Room, Laity Lodge, and A Rocha. The interwoven tapestry of these three with Art House would fill several chapters! Next book.

Finally, Margie and Denis Haack of Ransom Fellowship, Ned and Leslie Bustard of Square Halo Books, and Don Pape of Pape Commons are noted here for significant reasons. Like Steve Garber, Margie and Denis are the Christians Andi and Charlie wish everyone could know. Their wisdom and discernment are profound. The Bustards began as fans of Charlie, then friends of the family, and colleagues in publishing. You'll find Andi and Charlie contributing to several Square Halo titles, including *It Was Good: Making Art to the Glory of God* and *Wild Things and Castles in the Sky*. Pape Commons is the writers' collective that accomplished publisher Don Pape curates as agent, friend, and lover of writers and good books.

CONTACTS FOR FURTHER EXPLORATION

Wedgwood Circle—entertainment creation and investment.
https://www.wedgwoodcircle.com/

Commercial Music program at Lipscomb University—music education.
https://www.lipscomb.edu/academics/programs/commercial-music-songwriting-or-production

Makoto Fujimura—world-renowned Japanese *nihonga* artist and culture-care apologist.

    https://makotofujimura.com/ and https://iamculturecare.com/

Steven Garber—globe-trotting scholar specializing in vocation, empathy, wisdom, and wonder.

    https://washingtoninst.org/author/stevengarber/

The Rabbit Room—a creative community cultivating and curating stories, music, and art.

    https://rabbitroom.com/

Laity Lodge—retreat center bearing witness to goodness.

    https://www.laitylodge.org/

A Rocha—global family of community-based conservation projects.

    https://arocha.org/en/

Denis & Margie Haack—sage Christians, imperfectly wonderful, no agenda but love.

    https://ransomfellowship.org/ and https://www.critique-letters.com/

Square Halo Books—faithfully encouraging and equipping through literature and art.

    https://www.squarehalobooks.com/

Pape Commons—discovering, gathering, and advocating for writers.

    https://papecommons.com

To contact Charlie and Andi directly, please use the button at charlie peacock.com where you may also subscribe to their email list.

NOTES

EPIGRAPH

1. Excerpt from *Hallelujah Anyway: Rediscovering Mercy* by Anne Lamott, copyright ©2017 by Anne Lamott. Used by permission of Riverhead, an imprint of Penguin Publishing Group, a division of Penguin Random House LLC. All rights reserved.

CHAPTER 1

1. David Wilcox, "Show the Way," Irving Music, ©1994.
2. Wendell Berry, "Writer and Region," in *What Are People For?: Essays by Wendell Berry* (New York: North Point Press, 1990), 85.
3. Mary Oliver, "Sometimes," in *Red Bird: Poems* (Boston: Beacon Press, 2008), 37.
4. Denis D. Haack, "A Stick Becomes the Staff of God: Reflections on Faithfulness in the Ordinary & the Routine," *Touchstone* 7, no. 1 (Winter 1994), https://www.touchstonemag.com/archives/article.php?id=07-01-021-f.
5. Os Guinness, *The Call: Finding and Fulfilling the Central Purpose of Your Life* (Nashville: W Publishing, 1998), 59.
6. George Matheson, "O Love That Wilt Not Let Me Go," lyric first published in the Scottish Hymnal (1885). Public Domain.

CHAPTER 2

1. Dorothy L. Sayers, *Are Women Human?* (Grand Rapids, MI: William B. Eerdmans, 2005), 68–69.
2. Bono, *Surrender: 40 Songs, One Story* (New York: Alfred A. Knopf, 2022), 47.

CHAPTER 4

1. Charlie Peacock, *New Way to Be Human: A Provocative Look at What It Means to Follow Jesus* (Colorado Springs: Waterbrook Press, 2004), 104.
2. Peacock, *New Way to Be Human*, 105.
3. Wendell Berry, *Hannah Coulter: A Novel* (Berkeley: Counterpoint, 2004), 82.

CHAPTER 5

1. Dallas Willard, "Live life to the Full," Dallas Willard (website), http://www,dwillard.org/articles/live-life-to-the-full.

CHAPTER 6

1. Os Guinness, *The Call: Finding and Fulfilling the Central Purpose of Your Life* (Nashville: W Publishing, 1998), 108.

CHAPTER 7

1. Malcolm Gladwell, *Blink: The Power of Thinking Without Thinking* (Boston: Back Bay, 2007).

CHAPTER 8

1. Robert Farrar Capon, *The Supper of the Lamb: A Culinary Reflection* (New York: Modern Library, 2002), 91.
2. Eugene H. Peterson, *The Contemplative Pastor: Returning to the Art of Spiritual Direction* (Grand Rapids, MI: William B. Eerdmans Publishing Company, 1980), 23.

CHAPTER 9

1. Tom Gjelten, "Can America's 'Civil Religion' Still Unite the Country?" NPR, April 12, 2021, https://www.npr.org/2021/04/12/985036148/can-americas-civil-religion-still-unite-the-country.
2. Jordan Weissmann, "The Decline of the American Book Lover," *Atlantic*, January 21, 2014, https://www.theatlantic.com/business/archive/2014/01/the-decline-of-the-american-book-lover/283222/.
3. Luci Shaw, "The Returns of Love," Luci Shaw (website), accessed August 25, 2023, https://lucishaw.com/lucis-poetry/the-returns-of-love/.
4. Salena Zito, "Taking Trump Seriously, Not Literally," *Atlantic*,

September 23, 2016, https://www.theatlantic.com/politics/archive
/2016/09/trump-makes-his-case-in-pittsburgh/501335/.

5. Kris Kristofferson, "The Pilgrim, Chapter 33," *The Silver Tongued
Devil and I*, Monument Records, Nashville, ©1971.

CHAPTER 10

1. Kate Harris, *Wonder Women: Navigating the Challenges of Motherhood,
Career, and Identity* (Grand Rapids, MI: Zondervan, 2013), 72.

CHAPTER 11

1. Stephen King, *On Writing: A Memoir of the Craft* (New York: Pocket
Books, 2001), 145, 147.

CHAPTER 12

1. Stuart Townend & Keith Getty, "In Christ Alone," Thankyou Music
(adm. by Capitol CMG Publishing, UK & Europe, adm. by Integrity
Music, part of the David C. Cook family), ©2001.

2. "Fast Facts: Preventing Adverse Childhood Experiences," CDC,
accessed August 25, 2023, https://www.cdc.gov/violenceprevention
/aces/fastfact.html.

3. CDC, "Adverse Childhood Experiences (ACEs): Preventing Early
Trauma to Improve Adult Health," Vital Signs, updated August 23,
2021, https://www.cdc.gov/vitalsigns/aces/index.html.

CHAPTER 14

1. Augustine of Hippo, *The Confessions of Saint Augustine*, 9:6–7.

CHAPTER 15

1. Fred Smith, "Organizing Genius," The Gathering, December 7, 2022,
https://www.thegathering.com/round-table/organizing-genius.

2. Charlie Peacock, "Experience," EMI Blackwood Music, Inc./SonyATV,
©1990.

3. Steven Garber, *The Seamless Life: A Tapestry of Love and Learning,
Worship and Work* (Downers Grove, IL: InterVarsity Press, 2020), 7.

4. Os Guinness, *The Call: Finding and Fulfilling the Central Purpose of
Your Life* (Nashville: W Publishing, 1998), 27.

ABOUT THE AUTHORS

Charlie Peacock is a Grammy Award–winning, Billboard chart–topping music producer, composer, and recording artist. He is a cofounder of the Art House, Wedgwood Circle, and founding director emeritus of the Commercial Music program at Lipscomb University. Charlie has produced music for film and television, including *A Walk to Remember*, Chris Cornell's "Misery Chain" from the soundtrack of *12 Years a Slave*, and "Hush," the title theme to the AMC drama *Turn: Washington's Spies*. Named by *Billboard's Encyclopedia of Record Producers* as one of the 500 most important producers in music history, Charlie is also a three-time recipient of the Gospel Music Award for Producer of the Year. His books include *New Way to Be Human*, *At the Crossroads*, and a contribution to *It Was Good: Making Music to the Glory of God*. Charlie is the senior music editor for *Christianity Today* and host of the CT Podcast *Music and Meaning*. He has been married to Andi Ashworth for nearly fifty years, and they have two grown, married children and four grandchildren.

Andi Ashworth is the author of *Real Love for Real Life: The Art and Work of Caring*. She is cofounder of the Art House in Nashville, where she served for over two decades through hospitality and mentoring, hosting a wide range of guests and organizations, including Bono, Blood:Water Mission, International Justice Mission, the Gathering, and the ONE Campaign. Andi holds an MA in theological studies from Covenant Seminary in Saint Louis. As editor-in-chief of the *Art House America* blog, she stewarded hundreds of essays from a variety of authors, such as Tish Harrison Warren, Steven Garber, Sandra McCracken, Russ Ramsey, and Luci Shaw. Andi is most recently published in *Wild Things and Castles in the Sky: A Guide to Choosing the Best Books for Children* and *A Book for Hearts & Minds: What You Should Read and Why*. She has been married to Charlie Peacock for nearly fifty years and they have two grown, married children and four grandchildren.